AQA Mathematics
Higher (Linear)

GCSE

Series Editor
Paul Metcalf

Series Advisor
Andy Darbourne

Lead Authors
Sandra Burns
Shaun Procter-Green
Margaret Thornton

Authors
Tony Fisher
June Haighton
Anne Haworth
Gill Hewlett
Steve Lomax
Jan Lucas
Andrew Manning
Ginette McManus
Howard Prior
David Pritchard
Dave Ridgway
Kathryn Scott
Paul Winters

Nelson Thornes

Text © Sandra Burns, June Haighton, Anne Haworth, Gill Hewlett, Steve Lomax, Jan Lucas, Andrew Manning, Ginette McManus, Paul Metcalf, Howard Prior, David Pritchard, Shaun Procter-Green, David Ridgway, Kathryn Scott, Margaret Thornton and Paul Winters 2012
Original illustrations © Nelson Thornes Ltd 2012

The rights Sandra Burns, June Haighton, Anne Haworth, Gill Hewlett, Steve Lomax, Jan Lucas, Andrew Manning, Ginette McManus, Paul Metcalf, Howard Prior, David Pritchard, Shaun Procter-Green, David Ridgway, Kathryn Scott, Margaret Thornton and Paul Winters of to be identified as author of this work has been asserted by them in accordance with the Copyright, Designs and Patents Act 1988.

All rights reserved. No part of this publication may be reproduced or transmitted in any form or by any means, electronic or mechanical, including photocopy, recording or any information storage and retrieval system, without permission in writing from the publisher or under licence from the Copyright Licensing Agency Limited, of Saffron House, 6–10 Kirby Street, London, EC1N 8TS.

Any person who commits any unauthorised act in relation to this publication may be liable to criminal prosecution and civil claims for damages.

This edition published in 2013 by:
Nelson Thornes Ltd
Delta Place
27 Bath Road
CHELTENHAM
GL53 7TH
United Kingdom

13 14 15 16 / 10 9 8 7 6 5 4 3 2 1

A catalogue record for this book is available from the British Library

ISBN 978 1 4085 2152 6

Cover photographs: Purestock/Getty and Steve Debenport/Getty
Page make-up by Tech-Set Limited, Gateshead
Printed in China by 1010 Printing International Ltd

Photograph acknowledgements

Fotolia: pages 12, 16, 17, 18, 19, 26, 27, 46 (bottom)
iStockphoto: pages 8, 9, 21, 43, 46 (top)

Contents

Introduction 4

Section 1 — 5

Fractions and decimals, Percentages, Representing data,
Indices and standard index form, Ratio and proportion,
Scatter graphs, Collecting data, Statistical measures, Probability

Section 2 — 14

Prime factors, Sequences, Fractions and decimals, Surds,
Working with symbols, Graphs of linear functions,
Equations and inequalities, Percentages, Indices and standard index form,
Real-life graphs, Formulae, Quadratics, Simultaneous equations

Section 3 — 23

Fractions and decimals, Angles and areas, Working with symbols,
Percentages and ratios, Area and volume, Equations and inequalities
and formulae, Properties of polygons, 3-D shapes, coordinates and graphs

Section 4 — 31

Fractions and decimals, Angles and areas, Working with symbols,
Percentages and ratios, Area and volume, Equations and inequalities
and formulae, Properties of polygons, 3-D shapes, coordinates and graphs,
Reflections, rotations and translations, Pythagoras' theorem,
Properties of circles, Measures, Trial and improvement, Enlargements,
Construction, Loci

Section 5 — 41

Fractions and decimals, Angles and areas, Working with symbols,
Percentages and ratios, Area and volume, Equations and inequalities
and formulae, Properties of polygons, 3-D shapes, coordinates and graphs,
Reflections, rotations and translations, Pythagoras' theorem,
Properties of circles, Measures, Trial and improvement, Enlargements,
Construction, Loci, Quadratics, Trigonometry, Vectors,
Simultaneous equations, Cubic, circular and exponential functions,
Transforming functions

Answers — 54

Welcome to GCSE Mathematics

This book has been written by teachers who not only want you to get the best grade you can in your GCSE exam, but also to enjoy maths. Together with Books 1 and 2, it offers you the opportunity to put your skills and knowledge into practice.

In the exam you will be tested on the Assessment Objectives (AOs) below. Ask your teacher if you need help to understand what these mean. The questions in this book focus on AO2 and AO3 type questions.

AO1 recall and use your knowledge of the prescribed content.

AO2 select and apply mathematical methods in a range of contexts.

AO3 interpret and analyse problems and generate strategies to solve them.

Each chapter starts with a list of topics that will be needed for the exercise that follows. The questions will draw on one or more of the topics listed, so you will need to decide what methods to use to solve the problems.

How to use this book

To help you unlock blended learning, we have referenced the activities in this book that have additional online coverage in *Kerboodle* by using this icon:

The icons in this book show you the online resources available from the start of the new specification and will always be relevant.

In addition, to keep the blend up-to-date and engaging, we review customer feedback and may add new content onto *Kerboodle* after publication!

You will see the following features throughout this book.

 The bars that run alongside questions in the exercises show you what grade the question is aimed at. This will give you an idea of what grade you're working at. Don't forget, even if you are aiming at a Grade C, you will still need to do well on the Grades G–D questions.

Hint

These are tips for you to remember whilst learning the maths or answering questions.

Study tip

Hints to help you with your study and exam preparation.

 Bump up your grade

These are tips, giving you help on how to boost your grade.

Section 1

Before attempting this chapter, you will need to have covered the following topics:

- Fractions and decimals
- Indices and standard index form
- Collecting data
- Percentages
- Ratio and proportion
- Statistical measures
- Representing data
- Scatter graphs
- Probability

All these topics will be tested in this chapter and you will find a mixture of problem solving and functional questions. You won't always be told which bit of maths to use or what type a question is, so you will have to decide on the best method, just like in your exam.

Example: The cumulative frequency diagrams show the times taken by 50 boys and 50 girls to run 100 metres.

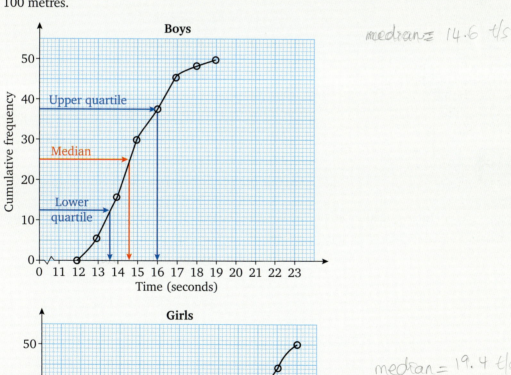

Compare the times taken by the boys and girls. *(6 marks)*

Solution:

> **Study tip**
>
> To compare two sets of data you must work out a measure of average and a measure of spread for each data set.
>
> When data is represented in the form of a cumulative frequency diagram, the best measure of average is the median and the best measure of spread is the inter-quartile range.

The median The median value is usually the $\frac{1}{2}(n+1)$th value.

In this case, $n = 50$ for both boys and girls.

Because n is large, the median value can be estimated from the $\frac{1}{2}n$th value (in this case the 25th value).

The median is approximately the time taken by the 25th runner.

The median time for the boys = *14.6 seconds*

The median time for the girls = *19.4 seconds*

Lower quartile Again, because n is large, the lower quartile (LQ) can be estimated from the $\frac{1}{4}n$th value (the 12.5th value).

The lower quartile is half way between the times taken by the 12th and 13th runner.

Boys LQ = *13.6 seconds*

Girls LQ = *17.5 seconds*

Upper quartile In a similar way, the upper quartile (UQ) can be estimated from the $\frac{3}{4}n$th value (the 37.5th value).

So the upper quartile is halfway between the times taken by the 37th and 38th runner.

Boys UQ = *16 seconds*

Girls UQ = *21.3 seconds*

Inter-quartile range The inter-quartile range (IQR) is the difference between the upper and lower quartiles.

IQR = UQ − LQ

Boys IQR = 16 − 13.6 = *2.4 seconds*

Girls IQR = 21.3 − 17.5 = *3.8 seconds*

Summary of measures Boys: Median = *14.6 seconds*, IQR = *2.4 seconds*

Girls: Median = *19.4 seconds*, IQR = *3.8 seconds*

Comparing the data sets The average time for the boys is smaller than for the girls. This means the boys are **on average** faster than the girls.

The inter-quartile range for the girls was greater than that for the boys. This means that the girls run **more variable** times than the boys.

> **Mark scheme**
> - 2 marks for calculating the median for the boys and the girls.
> - 2 marks for calculating the inter-quartile range for the boys and the girls.
> - 1 mark for saying that the boys on average are faster than the girls.
> - 1 mark for saying that the girls run more variable times than the boys.

Study tip

When you are asked to compare data sets make two statements. One comparing average values and one comparing measures of spread.

Average values

Use the word average in your statement. For example, 'boys run faster than girls' is wrong because boys only run faster on average.

Measures of spread

Show in your statement that you know that a smaller measure of spread means that the values in the data set are closer together. Useful phrases for this are 'less variable' and 'more consistent'.

Example: A council tax bill will be reduced by 5% if full payment is made before the end of April.

a Mr Akram paid £1350 on 1 May.
How much would he have paid if he had paid the previous day? *(3 marks)*

b Miss Wise paid £1539 on 27 April.
How much would she have had to pay four days later? *(3 marks)*

Solution: **a** To reduce by 5%, multiply by 0.95

1350 × 0.95

= £1282.50

Mark scheme
- 1 mark for using 95%
- 1 mark for multiplying by 0.95.
- 1 mark for the final correct answer.

Study tip

Use multipliers whenever possible. This is not the only way to reduce by 5% but when you are allowed a calculator it is the easiest method.

The calculator gave the answer as 1282.5. Remember that money should have two digits for pence. £1282.5 would not get full marks.

b £1539 is the amount that includes the 5% reduction.

So, 95% = £1539

1% = £1539 ÷ 95

= £16.2

100% = £16.2 × 100

= £1620

Mark scheme
- 1 mark for using 95%
- 1 mark for working out 1% then multiplying by 100.
- 1 mark for the final correct answer.

Study tip

This is known as a reverse percentage problem.
A very common error is to increase £1539 by 5%

Alternative Solution: **b** You can use a multiplier to find the reverse percentage in one easy step.

Divide by the multiplier:

£1539 ÷ 0.95 = £1620

Mark scheme
- 1 mark for using 0.95
- 1 mark for dividing by 0.95
- 1 mark for the final correct answer.

Study tip

For both parts you should check your answers.

In part **a** Mr Akram would have paid less if he had paid earlier so check that your answer is less than £1350.

In part **b** Miss Wise would have paid more if she had paid later so check that your answer is more than £1539.

AQA GCSE Mathematics Higher

1 Twenty miles per hour speed limit signs are put up on a housing estate.
The stem-and-leaf diagrams show the speeds of 15 cars both before and after putting up the signs.

Before						After					
1	9	9				1	6	8	8	9	9	9
2	4	6	9	9		2	0	2	3	4	6
3	0	0	2	6	6	3	2	5			
4	0	1	2			4	2				
5	2					5	1				

Key: 3 | 5 means 35 mph

Compare the speeds of the cars before and after putting up the signs.

2 School caterers ask pupils these questions.

a What is your age?

b How often do you buy a vegetarian meal?

c Pasta is healthier than chips.
Do you agree that we should stop serving chips?

Write a criticism of each of the questions asked.

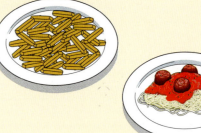

3 A mobile phone in Costlo is priced at £130.

The same mobile phone in Tescbury is priced at £155.

COSTLO PRICES EXCLUDE VAT

TESCBURY PRICES INCLUDE VAT

VAT rate is 17.5%

Compare the costs of the phone in the two shops.

4 The scatter graph shows the marks for ten students in French and German exams.

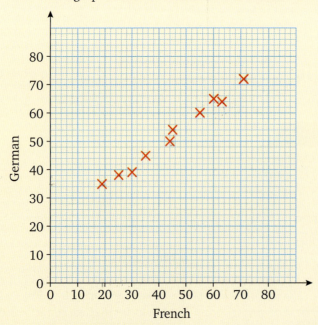

a Students who scored a total mark of 120 or more in both exams combined were awarded a certificate.
How many of the students were awarded a certificate?

b Sally was ill and missed the French exam but scored 60 marks in the German exam. Should Sally get a certificate? Explain your answer.

Section 1

5 Here is a recipe for cakes.

Sara wants to make some cakes for a children's party.

She decides to make 18 small cakes for the under-5s and 30 larger cakes for the older children.

Write a list showing the amounts of each ingredient that she needs.

You must show your working.

> **Ingredients for 24 small cakes or 12 larger cakes**
> 125 g of castor sugar
> 125 g of softened butter
> 125 g of self-raising flour
> 2 large eggs, lightly beaten
> 1 teaspoon of vanilla extract
> 2 tablespoons of milk

6 **a** Jenny spends $\frac{3}{8}$ of the money in her purse.
She has £17.65 left in her purse.
Work out the amount of money that Jenny spends.

b A team have won $\frac{2}{5}$ of their matches and drawn $\frac{1}{4}$ of them.
The team has lost 7 games.
A team scores 3 points for a win and 1 point for a draw.
A team scores no points when a game is lost.
How many points has the team scored?

7 In an experiment this trial was carried out a number of times.

> Take a bead at random from a bag containing 200 beads.
> Record the colour of the bead and then put it back in the bag.

The table shows the results from this experiment after 50 trials and after 300 trials.

Number of trials	Number of red beads obtained
50	11
300	78

a Calculate the relative frequency of the number of red beads after 50 trials.

b Work out the most likely number of red beads in the bag.
Show working to justify your answer.

8 The Angel Falls in Venezuela is 780 metres tall (to the nearest 10 metres).

What is its smallest possible height?

9 The number of pupils at a school increases from 750 to 780.

Work out the percentage increase.

10 PQRS is part of a number line.

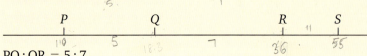

PQ : QR = 5 : 7

PR : RS = 4 : 1

P = 10

S = 55

Find the value of Q.

11 Each term Zoe takes tests in English, French and German. Last term her mean mark in the tests was 44.

Her target is to reach a mean mark of 50.

This term her mark in English improves by 10, but her mark in French decreases by 4.

By how much must she improve her German mark to reach the target?

12 Adam was saving his money for a games console that he had seen advertised in his local computer shop at a price of £280.

When he had saved exactly £280 he went to the shop to buy the games console.

The shopkeeper told him that the price had increased by 8% the previous week.

However, the shop had that day started a sale with a $7\frac{1}{2}$% reduction on all games consoles.

Did Adam have enough money to buy the games console?

You **must** show your working.

13 In a game, players throw two ordinary fair dice.
One of the dice is red and the other is blue.

Players can choose one of these options to obtain their score.

Option 1	Option 2
Add the numbers on the two dice.	Ignore the number on the red dice and double the number on the blue dice.

a Tom throws a 3 on the red dice and a 4 on the blue dice.
What are his possible scores?

b To win the game Charles needs a score of 10. Show that the probability Charles scores 10 on his next turn is $\frac{2}{9}$

c Charles actually throws 4 on the red dice and 1 on the blue dice.
Should Charles choose Option 1 or Option 2 to give himself the best chance of winning on his following move?

You **must** show working to justify your answer.

14 a Work out $10^2 + 10^1 + 10^0 + 10^{-1}$

b Work out $9 \times 10^{-2} + 8 \times 10^{-1} + 7 \times 10^0 + 6 \times 10^1 + 5 \times 10^2$

15 a Put these numbers in order of size. Start with the largest.

1.5×10^{-1} 2^{-3} 3^0 $0.25^{\frac{1}{2}}$

b The thickness of each page of a book is 5×10^{-3} centimetres.
The thickness of the front cover is 1.2 millimetres.
The thickness of the back cover is 1.2 millimetres.
The book has 70 pages.

Work out the thickness of the book.
Give your answer in centimetres.

16 a One person produces about 9×10^9 red blood cells in one hour.
How many million blood cells are produced by one person in one hour?

b The length of a bacteria cell is 2.5×10^{-4} millimetres.
The length of a red blood cell is 30 times the length of a bacteria cell.

Work out the length of a red blood cell.
Give your answer in standard form.

17 The map and table give some information about the continents of the world.

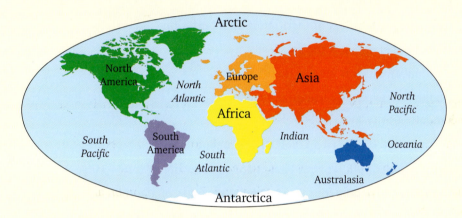

Continent	Population	Area (m²)
Europe	7.27×10^8	9.94×10^9
Asia	3.88×10^9	4.46×10^{10}
North America	5.02×10^8	2.43×10^{10}
South America	3.80×10^8	1.78×10^{10}
Africa	8.78×10^8	3.01×10^{10}
Australasia/Oceania	3.20×10^7	7.69×10^9

Population density $= \dfrac{\text{Population}}{\text{Area}}$

The table shows **all** of the populated continents.

Work out the average population density of all of the populated continents.

You **must** show your working.

18 There are 30 students in a class. The mean number of pets that they own is 0.8
No one owns more than 4 pets.

Copy and complete the table.

Number of pets	0	1	2	3	4
Number of students		12		2	1

19 Della buys a toaster for £35.20 in a sale. In the sale, prices are reduced by 20%

How much did the toaster cost before the sale?

20 A decorating company uses five workers to decorate six rooms in three days.
They have another job decorating eight different rooms of the same size.

They want to complete this job in two days.

How many workers should they use?

21 Here is a list of numbers.
4×10^7
8.5×10^{-3}
3.6×10^5
0.9×10^4
2×10^6
4.9×10^{-1}

a From this list write down:

  i the number which is **not** written in standard form

  ii the number which is the smallest

  iii a number which is greater than 1 million

  iv a number which is a square number.

b a and b are positive integers.

$a \times 10^b$ and $b \times 10^a$ are two numbers in standard form.

When written out in full $a \times 10^b$ has twice as many digits as $b \times 10^a$.

Show that there are only four possible pairs of values of a and b.

22 The table shows the percentage annual salary increase that a company has given to its employees over the past few years.

Year	2006	2007	2008	2009	2010
% salary increase	3%	6%	2.5%	1%	0%

a Before the 2008 increase John's salary was £25 000.
What is his salary in 2010?

b Carol joined the company in 2006. She did not receive the salary increase that year.
She left the company after the 2008 increase with a salary of £46 176.25.

  i Show that the percentage increase in her salary during the time she was working for the company was 8.65%

  ii Work out the salary she started with in 2006.
You **must** show your working.

23 Bruce ran for 21.8 seconds at an average speed of 7 metres per second.

The time is correct to the nearest tenth of a second.

The speed is correct to the nearest metre per second.

Work out the maximum distance that Bruce could have travelled.
Give your answer in metres.

24 Box A contains one blue and two red counters.
Box B contains two blue and one red counter.

One counter is taken at random from each box.

What is more likely:
the two counters are the same colour or the two counters are a different colour?

You **must** show working to justify your answer.

25 One hundred students run in a cross-country race.
The table shows the distributions of their times.

Time, t (minutes)	$20 \leq t < 25$	$25 \leq t < 30$	$30 \leq t < 45$	$45 \leq t < 60$	$60 \leq t < 70$
Frequency	4	12	42	33	9

a Draw a histogram to represent this information.

b The fastest 30 students receive a medal.
Estimate the time taken by the slowest student who receives a medal.

26 The table shows the number of people working different shifts at a factory.

Age		am	pm	Evening
Male	Under 30	6	8	9
	30 and over	7	12	17
Female	Under 30	8	11	18
	30 and over	6	15	23

A male worker is chosen at random and a female worker is chosen at random.

Work out the probability that they both work on the same shift.

Examination-style questions

1 A train company surveys opinions about the quality of its service.
On a particular train there are 140 passengers travelling standard class and 35 passengers travelling first class.
A sample of 40 passengers is taken, stratified according to the class of travel.

a Give one advantage of using a stratified sample in this situation. *(1 mark)*

b Calculate the number of passengers travelling standard class and the number of passengers travelling first class that should be in the sample of 40. *(3 marks)*

c Give another way in which the sample of passengers could be stratified. *(1 mark)*

AQA 2009

2 The number of mince pies sold by a bakery increases by 60% in December compared to November.
The number of mince pies sold in January is the same as the number sold in November.
Work out the percentage decrease in sales for January compared to December. *(3 marks)*

AQA 2008

Section 2

Before attempting this chapter, you will need to have covered the following topics:

- Prime factors
- Fractions and decimals
- Working with symbols
- Equations and inequalities
- Indices and standard index form
- Formulae
- Sequences
- Surds
- Graphs of linear functions
- Percentages
- Real-life graphs
- Quadratics
- Simultaneous equations

All these topics will be tested in this chapter and you will find a mixture of problem solving and functional questions. You won't always be told which bit of maths to use or what type a question is, so you will have to decide on the best method, just like in your exam.

Example: Tom, Lee and Sam are trying to win some marbles in a game.

Tom wins $\frac{2}{5}$ of the marbles.

Lee and Sam win the remaining marbles in the ratio 7 : 5

What percentage of the marbles does Lee win?

(4 marks)

Solution:

> **Hint**
> This is a multi-step problem. This means you have to plan your method.
> You are likely to gain more marks for your attempt if you work systematically, one step at a time, showing the method for each step.

You don't know how many marbles that Tom, Lee and Sam are trying to win but, because the answer required is a percentage, a good method is to assume that the number is 100.

It actually doesn't matter which number you choose but 100 makes the arithmetic in the problem much simpler.

Start by working out the number of marbles Lee and Sam win.

$\frac{2}{5}$ of 100 = 100 ÷ 5 × 2 = 40 marbles

100 − 40 = 60 marbles

or

$\frac{3}{5}$ of 100 = 100 ÷ 5 × 3 = 60 marbles

Next share the number of marbles won by Lee and Sam in the ratio 7 : 5

For every 7 marbles that Lee gets Sam gets 5.

7 + 5 = 12

So for every 12 marbles Lee gets 7.

60 ÷ 12 = 5

There are 5 lots of 12 marbles in 60 marbles.

5 × 7 = 35

So **Lee gets 35 marbles**.

Finally give the answer as a percentage.

35 as a percentage of 100 is 35%

So **Lee gets 35% of the marbles.**

> **Mark scheme**
> - 1 mark for working out that Lee and Sam have won 60 marbles.
> - 2 marks for working out that Lee gets 35 marbles.
> - 1 mark for the final answer.

Alternative solution:

First work out the fraction of marbles won by Lee and Sam.

$1 - \frac{2}{5} = \frac{3}{5}$

Then work out what fraction of these marbles that Lee wins.

7 + 5 = 12

Lee gets $\frac{7}{12}$ of the $\frac{3}{5}$ of the marbles.

Next calculate $\frac{7}{12}$ of $\frac{3}{5}$

$\frac{7}{12} \times \frac{3}{5} = \frac{21}{60}$

Finally change this fraction to a percentage.

$\frac{21}{60} = \frac{7}{20} = \frac{35}{100} = 35\%$

So **Lee gets 35% of the marbles.**

Example:

a Show that $\sqrt{80} + \sqrt{125} = 9\sqrt{5}$ (2 marks)

b Given that $(\sqrt{80} + \sqrt{125})^{-1} = \frac{\sqrt{p}}{q}$

Where p and q are integers, find the values of p and q. (3 marks)

Solution: For the first part of this question you have to change the form of the surds. Then you need to simplify.

a $\sqrt{80} + \sqrt{125} = \sqrt{(16 \times 5)} + \sqrt{(25 \times 5)}$

$\sqrt{(16 \times 5)} + \sqrt{(25 \times 5)} = 4\sqrt{5} + 5\sqrt{5} = 9\sqrt{5}$

> **Study tip**
> Always make sure that you write your answer in the space provided.

> **Mark scheme**
> - 1 mark is given for either $4\sqrt{5}$ or $5\sqrt{5}$
> - 1 mark is given for showing the addition $4\sqrt{5} + 5\sqrt{5}$

For part **b** you will need to use your answer to part **a**.

b Rationalise your answer to part a.

$$(\sqrt{80} + \sqrt{125})^{-1} = (9\sqrt{5})^{-1} = \frac{1}{9\sqrt{5}}$$

$$\frac{1}{9\sqrt{5}} = \frac{1}{9\sqrt{5}} \times \frac{\sqrt{5}}{\sqrt{5}} = \frac{\sqrt{5}}{9 \times \sqrt{5} \times \sqrt{5}} = \frac{\sqrt{5}}{9 \times 5} = \frac{\sqrt{5}}{45}$$

$p = 5, q = 45$

Hint
To rationalise your answer here, multiply the top and bottom by $\sqrt{5}$

Mark scheme
- 1 mark is given for $\frac{1}{9\sqrt{5}}$ this is a method mark.
- 1 mark is given for $\frac{\sqrt{5}}{9 \times \sqrt{5} \times \sqrt{5}}$ this is another method mark.
- 1 mark is given for $p = 5$, and $q = 45$

Questions

1 There are three piles of magazines.
Two of the piles are 30 cm high.
The other pile is 13.2 cm high.
Each magazine is 0.6 cm thick.
How many magazines are there in total?

2 Bill buys x packets of mints.
Each packet of mints cost 45 pence.
He pays with a £5 note.

a Write an expression, in terms of x, for the change that Bill should receive. Give your expression in pence.

b Bill receives £3.65 change. Write down and solve an equation to work out the number of packets of mints that Bill buys.

You **must** show your working.

3 The Ancient Egyptians used unit fractions like this: $= \frac{1}{3}$

A unit fraction has a numerator of 1.

The Ancient Egyptians made other fractions by adding unit fractions together.

For example, $\frac{2}{3}$ can be made by adding $\frac{1}{2}$ and $\frac{1}{6}$

$\frac{1}{2} + \frac{1}{6} = \frac{3}{6} + \frac{1}{6} = \frac{4}{6} = \frac{2}{3}$

Hint
You can use any pair of these fractions or all three.

a What other fractions can you make using $\frac{1}{2}, \frac{1}{3}$, and $\frac{1}{4}$?

b An Ancient Egyptian farmer shares 5 loaves between 8 people working in his fields.
   i   What fraction of a loaf does each worker get? Give your answer as two unit fractions added together.
   ii Describe how the farmer cuts the loaves to make sure each worker receives exactly the same amount.

c Repeat part **b** for 3 loaves shared between 4 workers.

Section 2   17

4 Ben has a collection of 210 DVDs.

Each of his DVDs is 14 mm wide.

He stores his DVDs in a special unit that has five shelves.

Each shelf is 700 mm long.

How many more DVDs can Ben store before the unit is full?

5 Each of these quantities has been rounded to the nearest whole number.

Write down the minimum possible size of each quantity.

   a   34 cm   **b**   60 kg   **c**   15 litres   **d**   £55

6

Three friends have some sweets.

They eat three-fifths of the sweets in the morning.

In the afternoon, the remaining sweets are shared equally between the three friends.

What fraction of the original number of sweets does each friend receive in the afternoon?

7 Last year Gordon ran his local marathon in a time of 3 hours and 10 minutes. Before this year's race he says:

'My target is to have a time that is at least 1% faster than last year.'

He runs this year's race in a time of 3 hours 7 minutes.

Did Gordon meet his target? You **must** show your working.

8 **a** The *n*th term of a sequence is $\frac{3}{2}n + 5$

       i Work out the first three terms of the sequence.

       ii Is 85 a term in the sequence? Show working to justify your answer.

    b Work out the *n*th term of the sequence

       3, 7, 11, 15, 19, ……

9 Fred has two dogs Misty and Millie.

Misty eats $\frac{1}{3}$ of a tin of dog food twice a day.

Millie eats $\frac{1}{2}$ a tin of the same dog food each day.

Work out how many tins of dog food Fred should buy for a week.

Each tin costs £1.15.

He has a voucher from his local store.

5p off each tin

when you spend over £20

Will he save money if he buys enough dog food for four weeks? Explain your answer.

10 p, q and r are prime numbers.

$1 < p \leq 4$

$7 \leq q \leq 9$

$10 \leq r < 15$

$x = pq$ and $y = qr$

Write down **all** the possible values of $x + y$.

11 You are given that $90 = 2 \times 3 \times 3 \times 5$

a Write 63 as the product of prime factors.

b Work out the highest common factor of 90 and 63.

c Write 900 as the product of prime factors.

> **Bump up your grade**
> To get a Grade C you need to be able to work out highest common factors.

12 x is an integer such that $-5 < 2x \leq 6$.

Write down all the possible values of x.

13 Dave and Debbie want to go out.
They can go to the cinema, an exhibition or a show at a theatre.
If they go to these they will need to travel by taxi each way.

	Distance from home	Ticket price per person
Cinema	8 miles	£8.50
Exhibition	6 miles	£10
Show	5 miles	£15.50

They have a choice of two taxi companies.

	Charge per trip
A2B Cabs	£2.60 per mile
Sapphire Taxis	£1.20 per mile plus £10

Use this information to work out which would be the cheapest option for them.

14 The diagram shows the graph of the equation $ax + by = 12$ where a and b are constants.

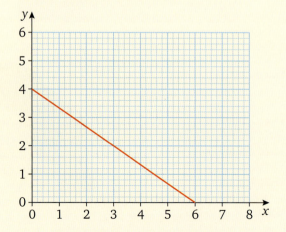

a Work out the values of the constants a and b.

b Work out the gradient of the line.

15 Solve:

   a $6(a - 2) = 2a + 16$

   b $\dfrac{d + 3}{2} = 5 - d$

Bump up your grade

To get a Grade C you must be able to solve equations that have brackets in them.

16 In an experiment, different weights, w, are attached to a spring.

The length of the spring, l, is then measured.

The graph shows the results.

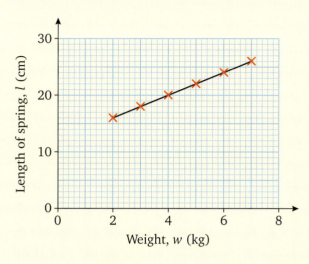

   a   Estimate the length of the spring when no weight is attached.

   b   Use the graph to write a formula to give the length of the spring, l, in terms of the attached weight, w.

   c   What weight is needed to **stretch** the spring by 30 cm?

17 Simplify:

   a $x^2 \times x^3$

   b $x^6 \div x^2$

   c $(x^2)^3$

   d $2x^2 \times 3x^3$

18   **a**   Show that $(x - 3)(x + 3) \equiv x^2 - 9$

   b   Hence simplify $\dfrac{x^2 - 9}{x + 3}$

19 Alfie, Ben, Colin and Dave share some money in the ratio of their ages.

Alfie and Ben together get $\frac{1}{4}$ of the money shared in the ratio 2 : 3

Colin has 40% of what is left.

Dave is 18.

How old are the other three boys?

20 Factorise fully:

   a $10x - 15x^2$

   b $5x^2 - x - 6$

21 Two lines, L_1 and L_2 intersect at P.

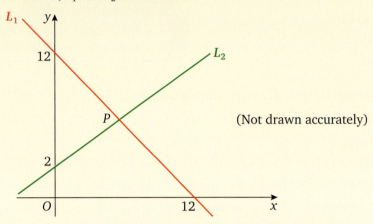

(Not drawn accurately)

The y-coordinate of P is twice the size of the x-coordinate of P.

a Show that the equation of L_1 is $y = 12 - x$

b Work out the equation of L_2.

22 Four friends Alana, Ben, Charlie and Della are playing a game.
During the game they collect red and blue cards.
The table shows the numbers of cards each player collects during the game.

Player	Red cards	Blue cards
Alana	10	8
Ben	11	4
Charlie	13	11
Della	9	2

a Each red card is worth r points.
Each blue card is worth b points.
Write an expression in terms of r and b for the total number of points won by Alana.

b Altogether Alana wins 64 points and Ben wins 80 points.
The player with the greatest total number of points wins the game.
Which of the four players wins the game?
You **must** show your working.

23 Solve the following simultaneous equations.

$2x + 5y = 16$

$4x + y = 5$

You **must** show your working.
Do **not** use trial and improvement.

24 x and y are integers.

$0 < x < 6$

$0 < y < 5$

$x + y \geqslant 7$

Work out the greatest possible value of $2x - y$.
You **must** show your working to justify your answer.

25 Look at this pattern.

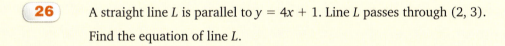

1^3 1 $= 1$ $= 1^2$ $= 1^2$

$1^3 + 2^3$ $1 + 8$ $= 9$ $= (1 + 2)^2$ $= 3^2$

$1^3 + 2^3 + 3^3$ $1 + 8 + 27$ $= 36$ $= (1 + 2 + 3)^2$ $= 6^2$

a Copy the pattern of sequences and add the next three lines.

b Describe the sequence of numbers in the middle column.

c Describe the sequence of numbers in the last column.

d Find the differences between successive numbers in the middle column and describe the sequence that they form.

e Use the ideas in the table to write down the value of $(1 + 2 + 3 + 4 + 5 + 6 + 7 + 8 + 9 + 10)^2$.

26 A straight line L is parallel to $y = 4x + 1$. Line L passes through $(2, 3)$.

Find the equation of line L.

27 **a** Here are five numbers.

3.6×10^6 4×10^{-2} 0.9×10^4 8×10^5 8.5×10^{-3}

    i Which number is **not** written in standard index form?

    ii Which is the smallest number?

b $a \times 10^b$ and $b \times 10^a$ are both written in standard index form.

When written out in full the number $a \times 10^b$ has twice as many digits as $b \times 10^a$.

Find four possible pairs of values for a and b.

28 You are given that $u = \sqrt{5} + 1$ and $v = \sqrt{5} - 1$

a $u + v = \sqrt{n}$

Work out the value of n.

b Find the value of:

$$\frac{uv}{u - v}$$

29 Make x the subject of the formula:

$$y = \frac{4(2 - 5x)}{2 - 3x}$$

30 Lipin thinks of a number.

She doubles the number and then adds it to the reciprocal of the number.

She gets the answer 3.

Write down and solve an equation to work out the **two** possible numbers that Lipin could be thinking of.

You **must** show your working.

Examination-style questions

1. A shopkeeper uses these formulae to calculate the total cost when customers pay by monthly instalments.

   $d = 0.2C$

   $C = d + 24m$

       C is the total cost in pounds.

       d is the deposit in pounds.

       m is the monthly instalment in pounds.

   The total cost of a sofa is £600.

   Work out the value of the monthly instalment. *(3 marks)*

   AQA 2009

2. 75 scientists are trapped in the Antarctic.

   They have enough food for 30 days on full rations.

   After 16 days on full rations a rescue party of 9 people arrive.

   The rescue party brings enough food to increase existing supplies by 60%

   The weather then gets worse and both the scientist and rescue party are trapped.

   They decide to go on half rations.

   How many more days before the food runs out? *(4 marks)*

   AQA 2008

3. a Work out $\frac{4}{5} \div \frac{6}{7}$

      Give your answer in its simplest form. *(3 marks)*

   b Work out $3\frac{3}{4} - 1\frac{2}{5}$ *(3 marks)*

   c Calculate the reciprocal of 0.5 *(2 marks)*

   AQA 2008

Section 3

Before attempting this chapter, you will need to have covered the following topics:

- Fractions and decimals
- Angles and areas
- Working with symbols
- Percentages and ratios
- Area and volume 1
- Equations and inequalities and formulae
- Properties of polygons
- 3-D shapes, coordinates and graphs

All these topics will be tested in this chapter and you will find a mixture of problem-solving and functional questions. You won't always be told which bit of maths to use or what type a question is, so you will have to decide on the best method, just like in your exam.

Example: A, B and C are three towns.

The bearing of A from B is 020°.
The bearing of A from C is 310°.
A and C are the same distance from B.

a Work out the angles marked x and y.
(3 marks)

b Work out the bearing of C from B.
(2 marks)

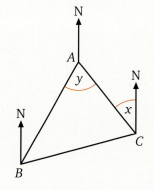

Not drawn accurately

Solution: **a** Firstly, mark on the diagram the information given in the question.
To do this, mark the 20° and 310° angles on the diagram.

Also, since A and C are the same distance from B, AB = AC

Mark the sides AB and AC with small lines to show they are equal.

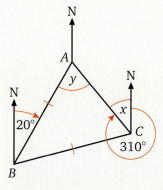

> **Study tip**
> Remember the bearing of A from B means you are **starting** from B, so the bearing is an angle **at** B.

The angle x must be 360° − 310° = 50°

So angle x is 50°.

You can now use interior angles to work out y.

Using interior angles, this angle must be 180° − 20° = 160°

Using interior angles, this angle must be 180° − 50° = 130°

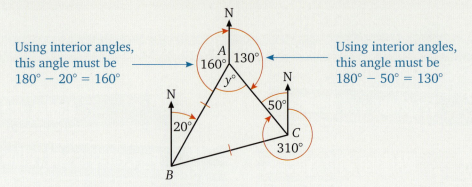

The three angles at A must add up to 360°.

So y = 360° − 160° − 130° = 70°

So angle y is 70°.

So the answer for part **a** is:

x = 50° and y = 70°

> **Mark scheme**
> - 1 mark for the angle x.
> - 1 mark for the angles of 20° drawn at B and 50° drawn at A.
> - 1 mark for the angle y.

b Think about which angle gives the bearing of C from B.

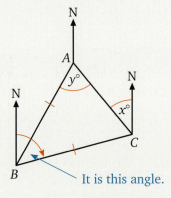

It is this angle.

So you need to work out angle ABC inside the triangle.

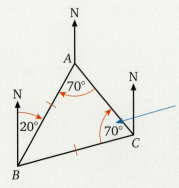

The triangle must be isosceles because we have already said that AB = AC. This angle must be the same as the angle at A.

The angle at C must be 70°.

Now you can work out the angle at B.

Angle B inside the triangle = 180° − 70° − 70° = 40°

Adding the angles at B, 20 + 40 = 60 so the bearing of C from B is 060°.

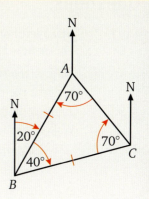

Study tip
Remember that your final answer must be a **three**-digit number, not just 60.

Mark scheme
- 1 mark for working out 40° at B.
- 1 mark for the final answer.

Example: The diagram shows one large circle, area L, and two small circles, each area S. They touch as shown. C is the centre of the large circle and is on the circumference of one of the small circles.

a Show that $L = 16S$. *(3 marks)*

b 16 of the small circles **cannot** be placed inside the large circle without any of them overlapping.
Give a reason why this is true. *(1 mark)*

Solution: **a** Let the radius of one small circle be r.

Use the diagram to work out that the radius of the large circle is $4r$.

$S = \pi \times \text{radius}^2$

$\quad = \pi r^2$

$L = \pi \times \text{radius}^2$

$\quad = \pi \times (4r)^2$

$\quad = \pi \times 16r^2$

$\quad = 16\pi r^2$

So, $L = 16S$

Study tip
There are no numbers to work with. Because you are asked to prove something, you should not use numbers for the radii of the circles.
Always make it clear what you are doing.

Study tip
A different letter can be used, e.g. x.
You must know the formula: area of circle = $\pi \times \text{radius}^2$
In $(4r)^2$, the brackets are necessary.
Remember to write expressions in their simplest form.
In some questions on circles, you need to use a calculator for the value of π. In this question the algebraic letter π can be used without needing to substitute a numerical value for it.

b Circles do not tessellate (they do not fit together with no gaps).

Study tip
The word tessellate does not have to be used but you must make your reason clear to the examiner.

Mark scheme
- 1 mark for using r and $4r$.
- 1 mark for obtaining $\pi \times (4r)^2$ or $\pi \times 16r^2$ or $16\pi r^2$.
- 1 mark for obtaining πr^2 and $16\pi r^2$.
- 1 mark for giving a correct reason.

Questions

1 Nisha left home at 9.00am to visit a friend.
This is how long her journey took.

Walk to the station	12 minutes
Wait for the train	21 minutes
Journey on the train	1 hour 15 minutes
Walk to her friend's house	12 minutes

a What fraction of the time was spent on the train?

b On the way back, the time for the whole journey took 15% less.

How long was the journey back?
Give your answer in hours and minutes.

2 The boat *Clarabel* breaks down and sends out a distress call.
The call is heard by two other boats, *Aramis* and *Bellamy*.
They set out to intercept *Clarabel*.
Aramis sets out on a bearing of 055°.
Bellamy sets out on a bearing of 260°.

Copy the diagram below and mark the position of *Clarabel*.

N

• *Bellamy*

Aramis •

3 Alice is four years younger than Ben. She is nine years older than Carly.
The total age of all three people is 79.

How old is Alice?

4 A rectangle has a length that is twice the width.
Four of these rectangles make this shape.

Work out the perimeter of the shape.

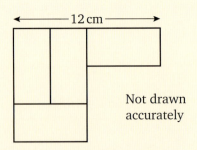

Not drawn accurately

5 The diagram shows the cross-section of a roof.
The two sides of the roof are perpendicular.
One side of the roof slopes at 35° to the horizontal.

The support is made from a rectangular piece of wood.
To make it fit, the wood is cut along the dotted lines.

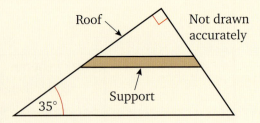

Work out the values of x and y.

6 To calculate a person's BMI this formula is used.

$$\text{BMI} = \frac{\text{weight in kilograms}}{(\text{height in metres})^2}$$

This table shows how people are classified using their BMI.

BMI	Classification
BMI < 20	Underweight
20 ≤ BMI < 25	Healthy
25 ≤ BMI < 30	Overweight
30 < BMI	Obese

a Ollie weighs 60 kilograms and is 1.8 metres tall.
Which classification is Ollie?

b Hannah is 1.54 metres tall. She weighs 68 kilograms.
Work out the least amount of weight that she must lose to be healthy.

7 An activity centre organises climbing trips for the public.

a Each member of staff at the centre must not take more than 8 members of the public in their group.
A party of 76 people book a trip.
12 members of staff are available to take the party.

   i Are there enough members of staff to take all the people?
You **must** show all your working.

   ii What is the ratio of staff to people for this trip?
Give your answer in the form $1 : n$

b In 2009 there were 18 726 people who went on climbing trips.
In 2010 this number increased to 19 871.

Work out the percentage increase.
Give your answer to one decimal place.

Bump up your grade
To get a Grade C you should be able to work out a percentage increase or decrease.

8 Three triangles fit together to make a parallelogram.

The base of the parallelogram is 10 cm long.
The area of triangle A is 28 cm².
The area of triangle B is 40 cm².

What is the area of triangle C?

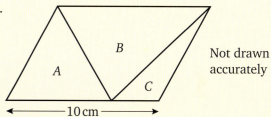

Not drawn accurately

9 Find an expression in terms of x for the area of this shape.
You must simplify your expression.

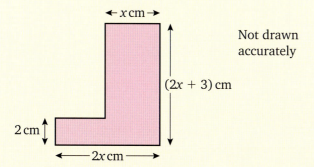

Not drawn accurately

10 The diagram shows a shape made by removing a semicircle from a trapezium.

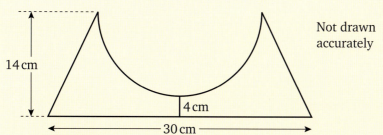

Not drawn accurately

Work out the area of the shape.

11 AB and CD are parallel lines.

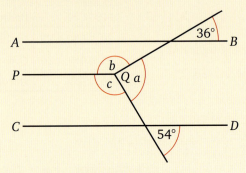

Not drawn accurately

a Show that angle $a = 90°$

b The ratio of angle b to angle c is $8:7$
Show that PQ is parallel to AB and CD.

12 A room contains a number of boys and girls. The ratio of boys to girls is $3:2$
When another 15 girls enter the room, the ratio of boys to girls changes to $2:3$

How many boys are there in the room?

13 **a** Work out the reciprocal of 8.
Give your answer as a decimal.

b Work out the reciprocal of 2.5
Give your answer as a fraction in its simplest form.

c Write down an expression for the reciprocal of $\frac{x}{2y}$

14 The points P, Q and R are on a straight line.

$PQ:QR$ is $3:1$

Work out the coordinates of point Q.

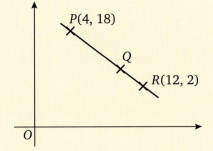

15 A 10 pence coin is approximately a cylinder of radius 12 mm and thickness 2 mm.

A vertical tower is made by stacking up £2 worth of 10 pence coins.

Calculate the volume of the tower.
Give your answer to the nearest cubic centimetre.

Not drawn accurately

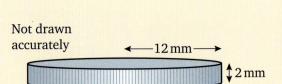

16 An interior angle of a regular polygon is 135°.
Another regular polygon has two sides fewer than this.

Work out one of the interior angles of this polygon.

17 Solve:

a $\frac{2x-1}{4} = 5 - x$

b $\frac{3x+2}{2} + \frac{2x-5}{3} = 1$

18 This tin of soup has height 14 cm and diameter 9.5 cm.
The label for the tin only covers the curved surface.
The label needs a 1 cm overlap to glue it down.

Calculate the area of the label in cm².

19 Expand and simplify $(c + 5)(c - 3)$.

20 A house was valued at £164 500 in 2005.
In each of the next two years the house increased in value by 6%
In the third year the value of the house decreased by 7.5%

Work out the value of the house after three years.
Give your answer to an appropriate degree of accuracy.

21 **a** Expand and simplify $(2x + 3)(x + 1)$.

b A rectangle has an area of 253 cm^2.
The lengths of the sides are integers greater than 1.

Using part **a**, or otherwise, work out the lengths of the sides of the rectangle.

22 In this cuboid, length : width : height = 4 : 1 : 1
The total surface area of the cuboid is 162 cm^2.

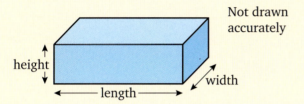

Not drawn accurately

Work out the volume of the cuboid.

23 **a** Simplify $(r + 2)^2 - (r + 1)^2$.

b The diagram shows three circles with the same centre O.
The radius of the middle circle is 1 m more than the inner circle.
The radius of the outer circle is 1 m more than the middle circle.

Show that the area of the outer band is $2\pi \text{ m}^2$ more than the area of the middle band.

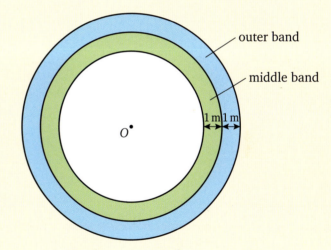

Not drawn accurately

24 A ball is dropped from a height, h metres.
It takes t seconds to reach the ground.
The height, h, is directly proportional to the square of the time, t.
It takes 10 seconds for the ball to reach the ground when dropped from a height of 490 metres.

If a ball takes 6 seconds to reach the ground, what height was it dropped from?

25 Here is a flow chart.

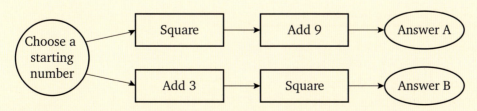

Samir says 'The difference between A and $B = 6 \times$ the starting number'

Prove that Samir is correct.

Examination-style questions

1 The graph shows a journey.

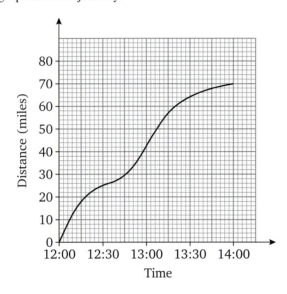

Work out the average speed of the journey.
State the units of your answer. *(4 marks)*

AQA 2008

2 The diagram shows the plan view of a landfill site on a centimetre grid.

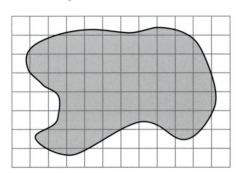

A landscape gardener is going to cover the site with turf (grass).
The table shows the cost of turf for different areas in (m²).

Area of turf (m²)	Cost per square metre
40 – 59	£2.83
60 – 130	£2.33
131 – 240	£2.03
241 – 480	£1.78
481 – 640	£1.53
641 – 960	£1.40
961 – 1440	£1.23

On the diagram one square metre represents 4 m².
The landscape gardener must buy enough turf to cover the landfill site.
Work out how much he has to pay.
You **must** show your working. *(3 marks)*

AQA 2009

Section 4

Before attempting this chapter, you will need to have covered the following topics:

- Fractions and decimals
- Working with symbols
- Area and volume 1
- Properties of polygons
- Reflections, rotations and translations
- Properties of circles
- Enlargements
- Angles and areas
- Percentages and ratios
- Equations and inequalities and formulae
- 3-D shapes, coordinates and graphs
- Pythagoras' theorem
- Measures
- Trial and improvement
- Construction
- Loci

All these topics will be tested in this chapter and you will find a mixture of problem solving and functional questions. You won't always be told which bit of maths to use or what type a question is, so you will have to decide on the best method, just like in your exam.

Example:

a Factorise $2r + \pi r$. *(1 mark)*

b Solve the equation $2r + \pi r = 21$
Give your answer to three decimal places. *(1 mark)*

c A prism with a semicircular cross-section is made by cutting out the shaded shape from an A4 piece of card. The dimensions of the card are 21 cm by 29.7 cm.

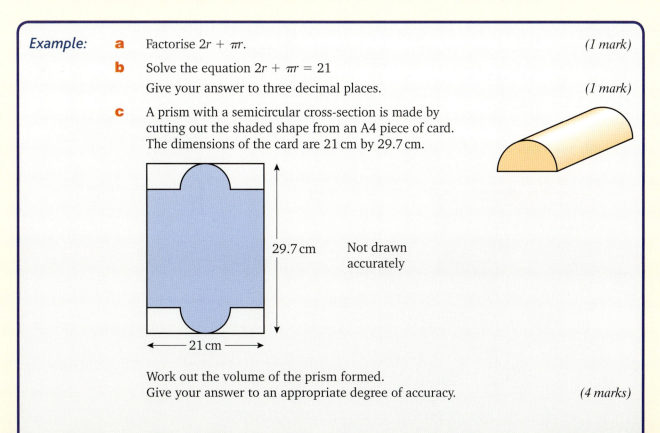

Work out the volume of the prism formed.
Give your answer to an appropriate degree of accuracy. *(4 marks)*

Solution: **a** Always begin by looking for common factors.

Here, r is a common factor.

$2r + \pi r = r(2 + \pi)$

> **Mark scheme**
> - 1 mark for factorising $2r + \pi r$.

b Use your answer to part **a**.

$2r + \pi r = 21$

$r(2 + \pi) = 21$

$r = 21 \div (2 + \pi)$

$= 4.084337...$

$= 4.084$ (to 3 d.p.)

> **Mark scheme**
> - 1 mark for working out r.

c Here, think about how you work out the volume of a prism.

volume of a prism = area of cross-section × length

The cross-section is a semicircle.

volume of a semicircular prism $= \frac{1}{2}\pi r^2 \times l$

You need to be able to find r, the radius of the semicircle and l, the length of the prism to solve this problem.

Think about how the flat shape folds up to make the prism.

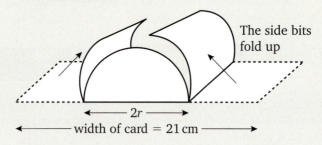

The side bits fold up

> **Study tip**
> One way of starting a problem is to try to work backwards.

> **Study tip**
> The formula of the volume of a prism would be given to you at the beginning of your exam paper.
>
> You need to learn the formulae to work out the area and perimeter of a circle and the area of a semicircle. From these, you can work out the area of a semicircle and the curved part of the perimeter of the prism in this question.

Together the side bits must be the same length as the curved part of the perimeter of the semicircle.

The curved part of the semicircle is worked out using πr.

Let the radius of the semicircle be r,

then $2r + \pi r = 21$

This is the equation you have solved in part **b**.

From part b, the value of r is 4.084

Now consider the length of the prism.

> **Study tip**
> When a long question is split into parts, keep looking back to the previous parts to see whether they can help.

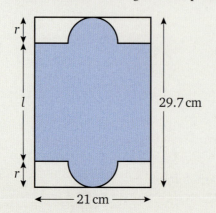

Let ℓ be the length of the prism,

$$\begin{aligned}\ell &= 29.7 - 2r\\ &= 29.7 - 2 \times 4.084\\ &= 21.53 \text{ cm}\end{aligned}$$

$$\begin{aligned}\text{Volume} &= \tfrac{1}{2}\pi r^2 \ell\\ &= \tfrac{1}{2} \times \pi \times 4.084^2 \times 21.53\\ &= 564.07\\ &= 560 \text{ cm}^3 \text{ (to 2 s.f.)}\end{aligned}$$

Mark scheme
- 1 mark for setting up the equation $2r + \pi r = 21$
- 1 mark for setting up the equation $\ell = 29.7 - 2r$
- 1 mark for using $\tfrac{1}{2}\pi r^2 \times \ell$.
- 1 mark for the correct answer to the appropriate accuracy.

Study tip
Remember that you will lose out on a mark if you do not round your answer to an appropriate degree of accuracy when the examiner has asked you to do so.

Example: In the diagram ABE, ADF, DCE and FCB are straight lines.

A, B, C and D lie on the circle.

Angle $DCF = 57°$

Angle CFD is twice angle BEC.

Work out the value of x. (4 marks)

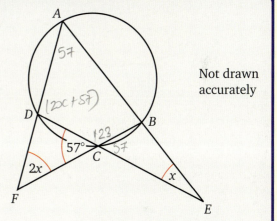

Not drawn accurately

Solution: Use the fact that the exterior angle of a triangle equals the sum of the opposite two interior angles.

Angle ADC must be $57° + 2x$

Angles on a straight line add up to $180°$.

Angle DCB must be $180° - 57° = 123°$

Opposite angles in a cyclic quadrilateral add up to $180°$.

As $ABCD$ is a cyclic quadrilateral, angles DAB and DCB must add up to $180°$ because they are opposite.

Angle DAB must be $180° - 123° = 57°$

Now add up the angles in triangle ADE.

The sum of the angles must be $180°$.

$$\begin{aligned}57° + (57° + 2x) + x &= 180°\\ 114° + 3x &= 180°\\ 3x &= 66°\\ x &= 22°\end{aligned}$$

Study tip
Look at the diagram and shapes and think about which theorems are relevant.

Here we have a cyclic quadrilateral and triangles. You know that:
- opposite angles of a cyclic quadrilateral add up to 180°
- angles of a triangle add up to 180°.

Try to see how many angles you can find in the diagram.

Mark scheme
- 1 mark for angle ADC $(57 + 2x)$.
- 1 mark for angle BAD $(57°)$.
- 1 mark for forming the equation.
- 1 mark for the correct final answer.

Questions

1 The diagram shows a centimetre grid with the points A, B, C and D marked.

On a copy of the grid draw:

a the locus of the point that moves so that it is an equal distance from A and B

b the locus of the point that moves so that it is an equal distance from A and C

c the locus of the point that moves so that it is an equal distance from C and D.

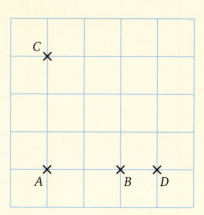

2 Which of these two shapes has the bigger area? You must explain your answer.

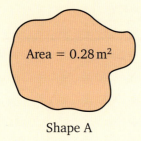

Shape A

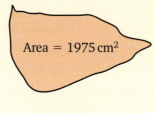

Shape B

Not drawn accurately

3 A quadrilateral has interior angles of x, $2x$, $(x + 35°)$ and $(x + 55°)$.

What is the value of x?

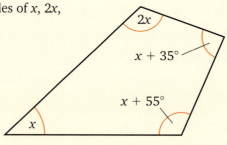

Not drawn accurately

4 The diagram shows a sketch of a triangular field, ABC.

a Using ruler and compasses only, construct an accurate scale drawing of the triangle.
Use a scale of 1 cm to 10 metres.

b In the field there is a telegraph pole. The telegraph pole is 44 metres from A and 63 metres from C.
How far is the telegraph pole from B?

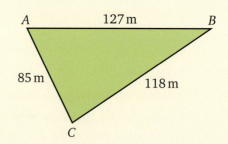

Not drawn accurately

5 These two right-angled triangles have the same area. What is the ratio $x:y$?

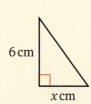

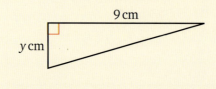

Not drawn accurately

6 A two-dimensional shape has the following properties.

> It has exactly one line of symmetry.
> It has exactly one reflex angle.
> The sum of all its interior angles is 360°.

One side of the shape has been drawn on the grid below.

Copy and complete the shape.

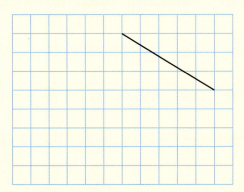

7 Write down two different transformations which map A onto B.

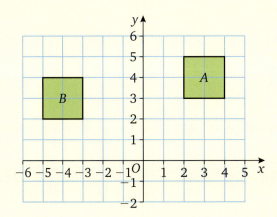

8 The diagram shows an irregular hexagon drawn on a centimetre square grid.
The dotted line shows an enlargement of one of the sides of the hexagon.

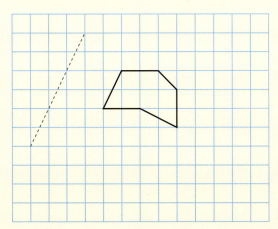

    a Copy the diagram and complete the enlargement.

    b Mark the centre of enlargement on the grid.

    c Write down the scale factor of the enlargement.

9 **a** Show that the perimeter and the area of this triangle have the same numerical value.

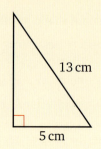

b This triangle has integer lengths. The numerical value of its perimeter and area are also the same.

Work out *x* and *y*. Show working to justify your answer.

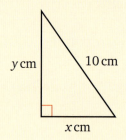

10 Wayne is driving on a motorway. After $2\frac{1}{2}$ hours he has travelled 125 miles.

a What is his average speed?

b Wayne sees this sign.

How long will it take Wayne to reach the services if he continues at his average speed?
Give your answer in minutes.

SERVICES 20 miles

11 $AB = x$ cm
BC is three times longer than AB.
CD is 2 cm longer than BC.

The perimeter of the shape is $2(4x + 3)$ cm.

Work out the length of AD in terms of x.

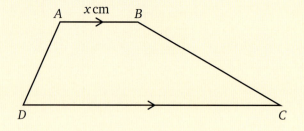

12 Oliver is downloading a file from the internet.
The file is 11.25 megabytes. The file downloads at a rate of 120 kilobytes per second.
There are 1024 kilobytes in a megabyte.

How long will it take to download the file?

13 **a** On the grid below, draw the line $y = x$

b Reflect the shape A in the line $y = x$

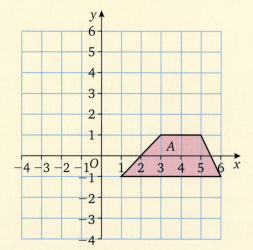

14 The volume of this cuboid is 480 cm³. Its height is 6 cm and its length is 5 cm.

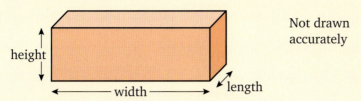

Not drawn accurately

The shape is cut down the middle along the dotted lines and then glued together to make a new cuboid.

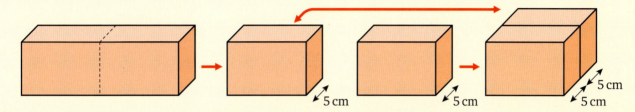

Not drawn accurately

The surface area of the original cuboid is 412 cm².
Melissa says that the surface area of the new cuboid is the same as the original one.

Is Melissa correct? You **must** show all your working.

15 A machine cuts circular discs of diameter 5 cm from a sheet of rectangular plastic.
The dimensions of the sheet of plastic are 1.2 m by 0.8 m.
The machine leaves the following horizontal and vertical gaps:

- 2 mm between each disc
- 2 mm gaps between the first row of discs and the top of the sheet
- 2 mm between the first column of discs and the left side of the sheet.

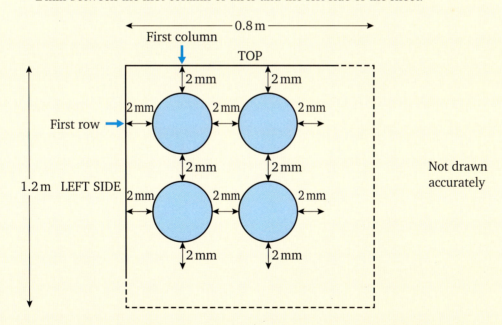

Not drawn accurately

a Show that 23 discs can be cut in each column.

b The unused part of a sheet is recycled. What percentage of a sheet is this?

16 A rectangle has length x^2 and width $x + 3$.
The area of the rectangle is 40 cm².

Use trial and improvement to work out the value of x.

Give your answer to two decimal places.

17 Tim and Sara are solving an equation using the method of trial and improvement.
They find the solution lies between 2.641 and 2.648

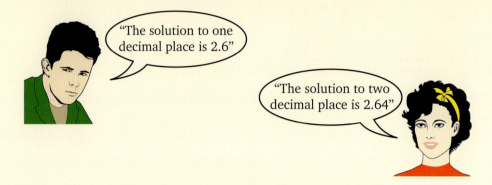

For each of Tim and Sara, which one of the following applies to their solutions?

- Definitely right
- Definitely wrong
- There is not enough information to tell

Give a reason for your answers.

18 Can either of these triangles be drawn inside a semicircle with the point *X* touching the semicircle as shown?

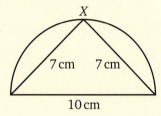 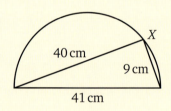

Not drawn accurately

You **must** show all your working.

19 In 2007 a bar of Yummichoc weighed 150 g and cost 85p.
In 2009 a bar of Yummichoc weighed 145 g and cost 95p.

a Work out the cost of 1 g of Yummichoc in 2007.

b What has been the percentage increase in the cost of a bar of Yummichoc, taking into account the increase in price and the reduction in weight?

20 A piece of wire 20 cm long is bent into a complete semicircle.

What is the area of the semicircle?

21 Each side of this hexagon is 6 cm long.
The angles *BCD* and *EFA* are right angles.

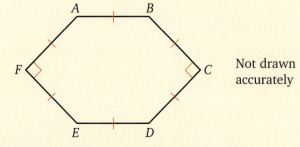

Not drawn accurately

Work out the area of the hexagon.

Section 4

22 The diagram shows the cross-section of a large vertical satellite dish.

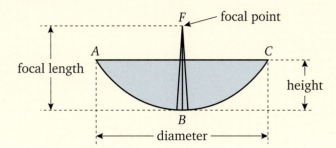

The curved part of the cross-section of the dish has the equation $y = \dfrac{(x-10)^2}{25}$
where $0 \leq x \leq 20$ and x and y are measured in metres.

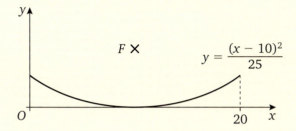

a Work out the height of the dish.

b Explain why the diameter of the dish is 20 m.

c The focal ratio of the dish is given by the formula:

$$\text{focal ratio} = \dfrac{\text{focal length}}{\text{diameter}}$$

The dish has a focal ratio of 0.3125

What are the coordinates of the focal point, F?

23 In the diagram ABP and DCP are straight lines.
$AC = AD$, angle $CAD = 28°$ and angle $BPC = 40°$

Work out the values of x and y.

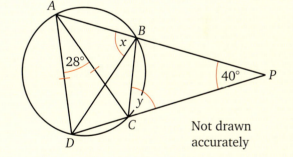

Not drawn accurately

24 The formula $\dfrac{1}{u} + \dfrac{1}{v} = \dfrac{1}{f}$ is used with lenses.

u is the distance of an object from a lens.
v is the distance of the image from the lens.
f is the focal length of the lens.
All distances are in the same units.

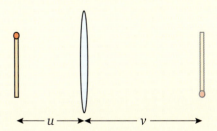

a Show that the formula can be rearranged into the form:

$$v = \dfrac{uf}{u-f}$$

b An object is placed in front of the lens at a distance that is twice the focal length. The distance of the object from the lens, u, is equal to $2f$.
Show that the distance of the image from the lens, v, is equal to u.

25 In 2010 the price of a ticket to a garden party was increased by 10% on its 2009 price.
The money raised from sales of tickets was the same as in 2009.

What was the percentage decrease in sales of tickets?

26 ABCD is a parallelogram.
P and Q are two points on CD so that CP = CB and DQ = DA
Angle DAQ = x

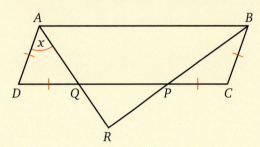

Not drawn accurately

a Express the following angles in terms of x.
  i Angle RAB
  ii Angle BCP
b Prove that angle ARB is a right-angled triangle.

Examination-style questions

1 ABCD is a cyclic quadrilateral.
PCQ is a tangent at C.
O is the centre of the circle.
Triangle ABC is isosceles.

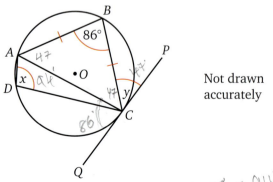

Not drawn accurately

a Work out the value of x. (2 marks)
b **i** Work out the value of y. (3 marks)
  ii Write down the name of the circle theorem used in part **b i**. (1 mark)

AQA 2008

＃ Section 5

Before attempting this chapter, you will need to have covered the following topics:

- Fractions and decimals
- Working with symbols
- Area and volume 1
- Properties of polygons
- Reflections, rotations and translations
- Properties of circles
- Trial and improvement
- Construction
- Quadratics
- Vectors
- Cubic, circular and exponential functions
- Area and volume 2
- Angles and areas
- Percentages and ratios
- Equations and inequalities and formulae
- 3-D shapes, coordinates and graphs
- Pythagoras' theorem
- Measures
- Enlargements
- Loci
- Trigonometry 1
- Simultaneous equations
- Trigonometry 2
- Transforming functions

All these topics will be tested in this chapter and you will find a mixture of problem solving and functional questions. You won't always be told which bit of mathematics to use or what type a question is, so you will have to decide on the best method, just like in your exam.

Example: In the diagram, the lines AC and BD intersect at E.

AB and DC are parallel and AB = DC

Prove that triangles ABE and CDE are congruent.

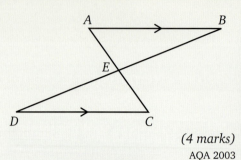

(4 marks)
AQA 2003

Solution: To prove that a pair of non-right angled triangles are congruent, one of these conditions has to be met:

ASA (Two angles and a corresponding side are equal.)

SSS (Three sides are equal.)

SAS (Two sides and the angle between them.)

> **Study tip**
> A useful first step in trying to prove that two triangles are congruent is to write down the conditions for any two triangles to be congruent.
> Then try to decide the one that is most likely to apply to the question.

In the question you are told that AB and CD are equal. So you know that one pair of sides are equal.

You are also told that AB and CD are parallel. This fact can be used to show that pairs of angles in the triangles are equal.

AB = CD   This is given in the question.
Angle ABE = Angle CDE   They are alternate angles.
Angle EAB = Angle ECD   They are alternate angles.

> **Study tip**
> Try to set your proof out a step at a time.
> Give a reason why each step is true.

So triangles ABE and CDE are congruent by ASA.

It would also be possible to state that:

Angle AEB = Angle CED   They are vertically opposite.

> **Mark scheme**
> 1 mark for noting that AB = CD and choosing a correct method.
> - 1 mark for saying angle ABE = angle CDE and why.
> - 1 mark for angle EAB = angle ECD and why.
> - 1 mark for the final correct statement.

Example: The diagram shows a circle of radius 8 centimetres, centre O.

A and B are points on the circumference of the circle that form a triangle with O.

Angle AOB is 120°.

Work out the area of the shaded segment.

Give your answer to an appropriate degree of accuracy.

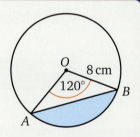

(4 marks)

Solution: The shaded area = area of sector AOB – area of triangle AOB

The angle AOB is 120° so the sector is $\frac{120}{360}$ (= $\frac{1}{3}$) of the circle.

The area of a sector with an angle of $\theta°$ is $\frac{\theta}{360} \times \pi r^2$

Area of sector = $\frac{120}{360} \times \pi \times 8^2$ = 67.0206... cm²

> **Study tip**
> Do not round your answer too soon as this might affect your final answer. Work out the area of the sector to at least six significant figures.

Area of triangle = $\frac{1}{2}ab \sin C$
Area of triangle = $\frac{1}{2} \times 8 \times 8 \times \sin 120°$
= 27.7128…cm²

Shaded area = 67.0206…cm² − 27.7128…cm²
= 39.3078…cm²
= 39.3cm² (3 s.f.)

Study tip

In the question you were asked to give your answer to an appropriate degree of accuracy. Here three significant figures are appropriate. 39 cm³ (rounded to the nearest whole number) would also gain a mark.

Mark scheme
- 1 mark for $\frac{120}{360} \times \pi \times 8 \times 8$
- 1 mark for $\frac{1}{2} \times 8 \times 8 \times \sin 120°$
- 1 mark for subtracting the triangle's area from the sector's area.
- 1 mark for the correct final answer.

Questions

1 A rectangle has a perimeter of $14x$ cm and an area of $12x^2$ cm².

Work out the length and width of the rectangle in terms of x.

2 This diagram represents an acre.
The acre is used to measure large areas of land.

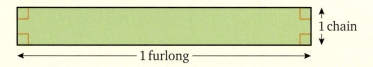

The metric unit for measuring large areas is the hectare.

1 hectare is approximately 2.5 acres.

1 furlong = 10 chains

1 chain = 22 yards

Use these values to estimate the number of square yards in 1 hectare.

3 The price of tickets for a boat trip to the Farne Islands is:

| Adults | £12 |
| Children | £8 |

On one of the trips, there are x adults and y children.

£T is the total price of their tickets.

a Write a formula for T in terms of x and y.

b On one boat trip, the total price of the tickets is £672.
The number of children's tickets sold is 18.
How many adult tickets are sold on this trip?

4 *ABCDEF* is a regular hexagon with centre *O*.
The hexagon is divided into congruent triangles.
G is the midpoint of *AB*.
H is the midpoint of *ED*.
Two triangles, *X* and *Y*, are labelled.

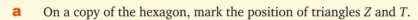

Triangle *X* maps onto triangle *Z* by a rotation of 180° about *O* followed by a reflection in the line *BD*.
Triangle *X* maps onto triangle *Y* by a translation onto triangle *T* followed by a reflection.

a On a copy of the hexagon, mark the position of triangles *Z* and *T*.

b Describe fully the single transformation that maps triangle *T* onto triangle *Y*.

5 Orange squash is made by mixing concentrated orange juice with water.

Holly is making some orange squash.

She has poured 50 millilitres of concentrated orange juice into a cylindrical glass.

The graph shows what happens next.

a Describe fully what is happening during the first three seconds.

b Write the ratio of concentrated orange juice to water in its simplest form when the orange squash has been made.

c For how many seconds was Holly drinking squash from the glass?

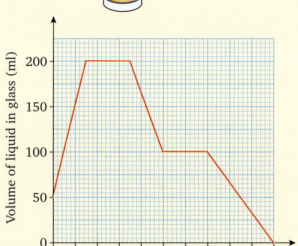

6 Here are details of Sudhir's bicycle journey.

Stage 1: After the start he cycles at a speed of 12 km/h for $2\frac{1}{2}$ hours.

Stage 2: He stops for 30 minutes.

Stage 3: He cycles back towards the start for 1 hour, travelling 10 km.

Stage 4: He stops for another 30 minutes.

Stage 5: He cycles back to the start at a speed of 8 km/h.

On a copy of these axes, draw a distance–time graph to represent Sudhir's journey.

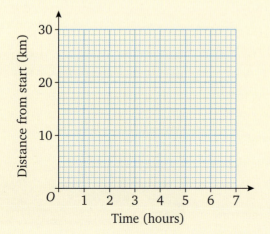

7 There are some red counters, white counters and blue counters in a bag.
There are 50% more white counters than red counters.
The number of blue counters is three-fifths of the number of white counters.

Write the ratio of the numbers of red to white to blue counters in its simplest form.

> **Study tip**
>
> Although you can use an algebraic method to solve a question like this, sometimes it can be easier to solve it by choosing a particular number (100 is best) for the red counters and then working out the others from this number.

8 **a** The perimeter of this rectangle is $8x + 4$.

Write down an expression for the area of this rectangle.

b Write down an expression for the area of a square with perimeter $8x + 4$.

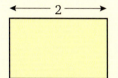

9 In a test there are 10 questions.
If you attempt a question and get it right, you score 5 marks.
If you attempt a question and get it wrong, you lose 2 marks.
If you do **not** attempt a question, you lose 10 marks.

a The table shows how three friends, Andrew, Bill and Clare, do in the test.

Name	Number of questions attempted	Number of questions correct
Andrew	10	6
Bill	9	8
Clare	8	7

In the test the mark for a Merit is 30.
The mark for a Pass is 20.

How well do the three friends do in the test?
You must show working to justify your answer.

b Tim takes the test.
He scores -7.

How many questions did Tim **not** attempt?
You must show working to justify your answer.

10 **a** Rachel tries to draw a quadrilateral with exactly three interior right angles.
Explain why she finds this impossible.

b Tom says that he can draw a hexagon with exactly five interior right angles.
Is this possible?
Show working to justify your answer.

11 Work out the coordinates of the point where the graph of $y = 2x - 3$ intersects the graph of $x + 2y = 4$.

12 Plot the points $A(1, 2)$, $B(4, 1)$ and $C(2, 0)$ on a centimetre grid.

a Show that $AC = BC$.

b Draw the locus of points that are equidistant from A and B.

13 In box A there are x beads.
In box B there are two more beads than in box A.
In box C there are three times as many beads as there are in box B.
In box D there are five times as many beads as there are in box A.
In box E there are four more beads than there are in box D.

Show that the total number of beads in boxes A, B, C and D is double the number of beads in box E.

14 Use trial and improvement to find a solution to the equation $x^3 - 2x = 45$

The table shows the first trial.

x	$x^3 - 2x$	Conclusion
3	$3^3 - 2 \times 3 = 21$	too small

Continue the table to find a solution to the equation.
Give your answer to one decimal place.

15 Adil and James are planning a mountain walk.

They find this rule to help them estimate how long the walk will take.

> Estimating the time of a mountain walk
>
> On a mountain walk it takes:
>
> 1 hour for every 3 miles travelled horizontally
>
> *plus*
>
> 1 hour for every 2000 feet climbed
>
> Add 10 minutes of resting time for each hour you walk

When planning their mountain walk, Adil and James estimate they will:
- travel 24 kilometres horizontally
- climb for 900 metres.

They plan to start their walk at 09:00.

At what time are they likely to complete their walk?

16 David has a large number of 2p coins.
He puts them into four piles: A, B, C and D.
In pile B there are 30 more coins than in pile A.
In pile C there are 12 times as many coins as there are in pile A.
In pile D there are 8 times as many coins as there are in pile A.
David notices that the total number of coins in piles A, B and D is equal to the number of coins in pile C.

What is the total number of 2 pence coins that David has?

17 This formula gives the stopping distance of a car travelling on a dry road in terms of its speed.

$$d = \frac{v^2}{150} + \frac{v}{5}$$

d is the stopping distance in metres

v is the speed of the car in km/h

a i Copy and complete this table of values for $d = \frac{v^2}{150} + \frac{v}{5}$

v (km/h)	0	15	30	45	60	75	90	105	120
d (metres)					36			94.5	

   ii Draw the graph of $d = \frac{v^2}{150} + \frac{v}{5}$ for values of v from 0 to 120.

b The stopping distance on a wet road is double that on a dry road.
Use your graph to answer these questions.

   i A car is travelling at a speed of 95 km/h on a wet road.
   Estimate its stopping distance.

   ii The speed limit on a motorway in the UK is 112 km/h.
   A car is forced to brake suddenly in wet conditions on a motorway.
   Its stopping distance is 240 metres.
   Was the car travelling within the speed limit?

18 The volume V of this square-based pyramid is given by the formula $V = \frac{1}{3}x^2h$ where x and h are measured in centimetres.

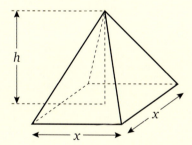

a Work out the volume of the pyramid when $x = 6$ and $h = 8$

b Aaron has been asked to make a square-based pyramid.
The height must be 2 cm bigger than the length of the base.
The volume of the pyramid must be 125 cm³.
He uses trial and improvement to work out the length of the base, x.

Complete his worksheet to find x to one decimal place.

Length of base, x (cm)	Height, h	x²	Volume (cm³)	
7	9	49	147	too big

19 **a** Work out the length x in this triangle.

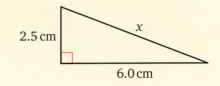

Not drawn accurately

b The diagram shows a 2-metre long ladder leaning against a vertical wall.

The ladder reaches 1.8 metres up the wall from the ground.
To use a ladder safely, the ladder should be inclined with a gradient of 4.

Is the ladder safe to use in the position shown?

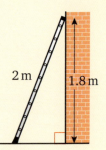

c The sides of an equilateral triangle are 12 centimetres long.

Work out the height, h, of the equilateral triangle.

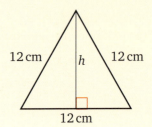

Not drawn accurately

20 *ABCDE* is a regular pentagon.

Prove that *ACDE* is a trapezium.

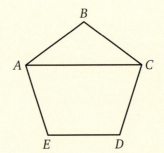

21 Work out the length of *CD*.

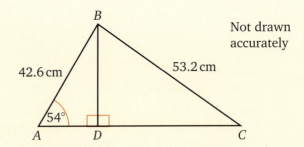

Not drawn accurately

22 Mrs Sim has this photo frame.

The photo frame is designed for a photograph of length 24 cm and width 17.5 cm.
Mrs Sim has a photograph of her daughter stored on her digital camera.
The print of this photograph has length 8 cm and width 5 cm.

Not drawn accurately

a Show that an enlargement of the print will **not** fit in the photo frame exactly.

b Mrs Sim decides to crop the 8 cm side of her print before enlarging.
What length should she make this side so that the enlargement will fit in the photo frame exactly?

23 The diagram shows a sketch of a field, ABCD.
AB = 64 metres and BC = 102 metres.
The bearing of B from A is 348°.
The bearing of C from A is 040°.
The bearing of D from C is 162°.
D is due east of A.

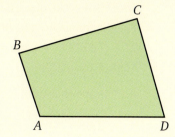

- **a** On plain paper make a scale drawing of the field.
  Write down the scale you have used.

- **b** A straight path from A is at right angles to CD.
  A straight path from B is always an equal distance from BC and BA.
  The two paths intersect at the point X.

  Using ruler and compasses only, construct both of these paths on your scale drawing of the field.

- **c** Billy runs along the path from A to X, then along the path from X to B in 30 seconds.
  Work out his average speed in metres per second.

24
- **a** Copy and complete the table for $y = x^3 - 3x - 5$

x	−2	−1	0	1	2	3
y		−3	−5			13

- **b** Draw axes with values of x from −2 to 3 and values of y from −8 to +14.
  On these axes, draw the graph of $y = x^3 - 3x - 5$ for values of x

- **c** Use your graph to solve $x^3 - 3x - 5 = 8$

25 Mrs Grey can buy four cakes and three drinks for £7.

If she buys two more cakes and one more drink the cost will be £10.20.

Work out the cost of one cake.

26 Here is a triangle.

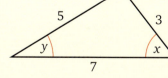

- **a** Show that the triangle cannot be right angled.
- **b** Explain why angle x is greater than angle y.
- **c** Which one of these six statements is correct?

  i $\dfrac{\sin x}{7} = \dfrac{\sin y}{5}$ **iv** $\dfrac{\sin x}{5} = \dfrac{\sin y}{7}$

  ii $\dfrac{\sin x}{3} = \dfrac{\sin y}{7}$ **v** $\dfrac{\sin x}{3} = \dfrac{\sin y}{5}$

  iii $\dfrac{\sin x}{5} = \dfrac{\sin y}{3}$ **vi** $\dfrac{\sin x}{7} = \dfrac{\sin y}{3}$

27
- **a** Factorise fully $w \times w \times 2 + w + w + w + w + 2$
- **b** Simplify $(x + 2)^2 - (x - 2)^2$
- **c** Prove that $\dfrac{1}{x - 1} + \dfrac{1}{x + 1} = \dfrac{2x}{x^2 - 1}$

28 ABCD is a cyclic quadrilateral.
The diagonals AC and BD intersect at X.
BX = 7 cm, CX = 4 cm and DX = 6 cm
Angle BXC = 138°

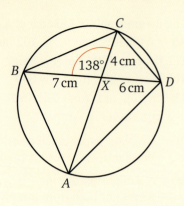

Not drawn accurately

a Prove that triangles BXC and AXD are similar.

b Work out the length of AX.

c Work out the length of BC.

29 The volume of a sphere is 288π mm^3.

Calculate the radius of the sphere.

30 Here is a triangle.

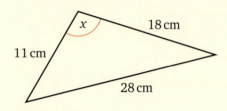

Not drawn accurately

Work out angle x.

31 ABCD is a quadrilateral.

$\overrightarrow{AB} = \begin{pmatrix} 3 \\ 1 \end{pmatrix}$ $\overrightarrow{BC} = \begin{pmatrix} 2 \\ -5 \end{pmatrix}$ $\overrightarrow{CD} = \begin{pmatrix} -5 \\ -2 \end{pmatrix}$

Prove that D is vertically below A.

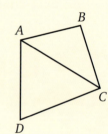

Not drawn accurately

32 Given that y is inversely proportional to x^2, copy and complete the table.

x	5	10		
y	5			500

33 $\overrightarrow{OP} = -2\mathbf{a} + 4\mathbf{b}$ and $\overrightarrow{OQ} = 4\mathbf{a} - 2\mathbf{b}$

a Express $\overrightarrow{PQ}$ in terms of **a** and **b**.

b R is the midpoint of $\overrightarrow{PQ}$.
Express $\overrightarrow{OR}$ in terms of **a** and **b**.

c $\overrightarrow{PS} = 7\mathbf{a} + \mathbf{b}$
Express $\overrightarrow{OS}$ in terms of **a** and **b**.

d What **two** facts do $\overrightarrow{OR}$ and $\overrightarrow{OS}$ indicate about the points O, S and R.

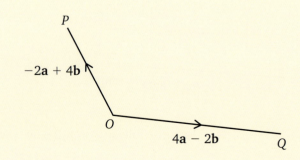

34 a Here are four equations.

A $y = \dfrac{3}{x}$ B $y = 3^x$ C $y = 3x$ D $y = x^3$

Match each graph to its equation.

i 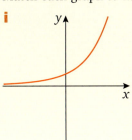 ii 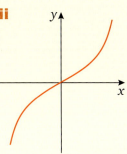 iii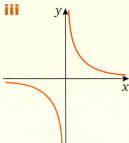

b Here is a sketch graph.

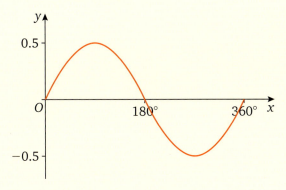

i Explain why this **cannot** be a sketch of the graph of $y = \sin x$ for values of x from $0°$ to $360°$.

ii Write down the equation of the sketch graph.

35 In triangle ABC, $AB = 5$ cm, $AC = 7$ cm and angle $ABC = 105°$

Work out the area of the triangle.

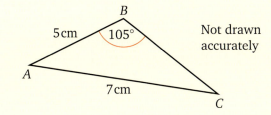

36 An oil container consists of a cylinder on top of a cone.
The diameter of the cylinder is 200 cm.
The height of the cone and the cylinder are both 100 cm.

Initially the container is full.
Oil flows from the container until it reaches a level 40 cm from the bottom of the container.

Work out the volume of oil that has flowed from the container.

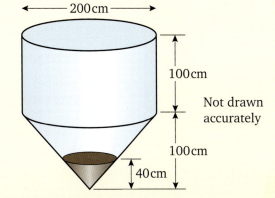

37 AB, BC and CD are straight lines.

$\overrightarrow{AB} = \begin{pmatrix} 3 \\ 5 \end{pmatrix}$ $\overrightarrow{CD} = \begin{pmatrix} 12 \\ k \end{pmatrix}$ angle ABC = angle BCD

Work out k.

Give reasons for your answer.

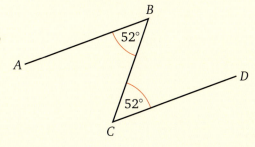

38 Describe fully the transformations that map the first graph to the second graph.

a $y = x^3$ to $y = x^3 - 4$

b $y = \sin x$ to $y = 2\sin x$

c $y = x^2$ to $y = (x + 1)^2$

39 The graphs of $y = x^2 - x - 3$ and $y = 2x + 1$ are shown.

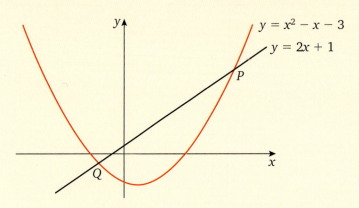

The graphs intersect at points P and Q.

Find the coordinates of the midpoint of the line PQ.

40 Here are two transformations.

Transformation A: reflect in the x-axis

Transformation B: translate 4 units vertically downwards

Holly applies transformation A to the graph $y = x^2$
She then applies transformation B to the graph she has obtained.

Tikram applies transformation B to the graph $y = x^2$
He then applies transformation A to the graph he has obtained.

How could Holly's final graph be transformed to Tikram's final graph?

41 A cylinder is filled with water to a depth of 3 cm from the top as shown.

Spheres of radius 4.5 cm are to be placed, one at a time, in the cylinder.
The spheres will sink in the water.

Work out the least number of spheres needed for the water to overflow from the cylinder.

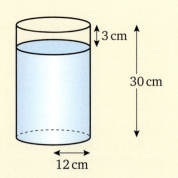

Not drawn accurately

42 A rectangle has a perimeter of 18.4 cm and an area of 21 cm².

Let the length of the rectangle be x cm.

a Show that $5x^2 - 46x + 105 = 0$.

b Work out the length and width of the rectangle.

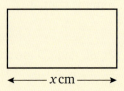

Examination-style questions

1 A triangle has angles of 80°, x and 4x.
Show that the triangle is isosceles.

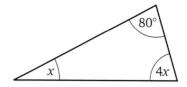

(4 marks)
AQA 2008

2 A and B are two similar cylinders.
The height of cylinder A is 10 cm and its volume is 625 cm³.
The volume of cylinder B is 5000 cm³.

Calculate the height of cylinder B.

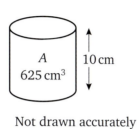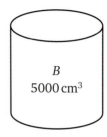

(3 marks)
AQA 2000

3 ABCD is a quadrilateral.
AB = 4.6 cm
BC = 6.9 cm
AD = 3.8 cm
Angle ABC = 90°
Angle CAD = 48°

Work out the perimeter of the quadrilateral.

Give your answer to an appropriate degree of accuracy.

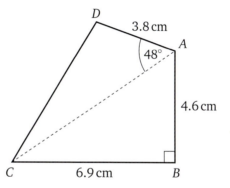

(5 marks)
AQA 2009

4 Sam has made some wooden play blocks for a nursery class.
Each block is a prism with an L-shaped cross-section.

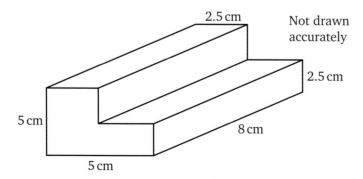

Sam paints the entire surface of the blocks with one coat of red paint.
Sam has enough red paint to cover 3000 square centimetres.

What is the maximum number of blocks that he can paint red?

(4 marks)
AQA 2009

Answers

Section 1

1. Median   Before 30 mph   After 22 mph
   Range   Before 33 mph   After 35 mph
   The smaller median indicates that on average the speed is less after putting up the road signs. The slightly greater range indicates that the speed through the housing estate is slightly more variable after putting up the signs

2. No age ranges given so there will be many different answers given.
   No response boxes – unclear whether asking per day/week etc.
   A leading question that is trying to gain a particular response.

3. Costlo £152.75 so cheaper than Tescbury even with VAT added on

4. a 3
   b No. Nearly all students scored fewer marks on the French test than the German test. So the total would be less than 120.

5. Sugar   406.25 (Allow 410 or 405)
   Butter   406.25
   Flour   406.25
   Eggs   6.5 (Allow 6 or 7)
   Vanilla   3.25 (Allow 3)
   Milk   6.5 (Allow 6 or 7)

6. a £10.59   b 29

7. a $\frac{11}{50}$ or 0.22
   b 52

8. 775 metres

9. 4%

10. 25

11. 12

12. Yes, the price is now £279.72

13. a 7 or 8
    b (r,b)
    Identifies (4,6) (5,5) and (6,4)   Using Option 1
    Identifies (1,5), (2,5) … to (6,5)   Using Option 2
    $\frac{8}{36} (= \frac{2}{9})$ Need to see 8/36
    c Option 1   Option 2
        Moves 5   Moves 2
        5 to go   8 to go
    Identifies outcomes or gives probability for the number of squares left $\frac{4}{36}$ $\frac{10}{36}$
    He should choose option 2 because scoring 8 on the next go is more likely than scoring 5.

14. a 110.9   b 567.89

15. a 3^0 $0.25^{½}$ 1.5 3 10^{-1} 2^{-3}
    b 0.59 cm

16. a 9000 or 9×10^3 b 7.5×10^{-3}

17. Total population = 6.399×10^9
    Total area = 1.3443×10^{11}
    $6.399 \times 10^9 \div 1.3443 \times 10^{-1}$
    4.76×10^{-2}

18.

Number of pets	0	1	2	3	4
Number of students	14	12	1	2	1

19. £44.00

20. 10

21. a i 0.9×10^4
        ii 8.5×10^{-3}
        iii 4×10^7 or 2×10^6
        iv 3.6×10^5 or 4.9×10^{-1}
    b $b + 1 = 2(a + 1)$ or $b = 2a + 1$
    Recognition of relationship between powers of 10 (1,3), (2,5), (3,7), (4,9)

22. a £25,881.25
    b i 1.06×1.025
       1.0865
       108.65% = 46 176.25
       ii $46\,176.25 \div 1.0865 = £42\,500$

23. 163.875 metres

24. $\frac{1}{3} \times \frac{2}{3} + \frac{2}{3} \times \frac{1}{3} (= \frac{4}{9})$ Blue and Blue or Red and Red
    $1 - \frac{4}{9} (= \frac{5}{9})$ Blue and Red or Red and Blue
    Different colour

25. a Frequency densities 0.8, 2.4, 2.8, 2.2 and 0
       Group widths 5, 5, 15, 15 and 10
    b 54.5 minutes

26. $\frac{13}{27} \times \frac{14}{26} + \frac{20}{46} \times \frac{26}{45} + \frac{26}{67} \times \frac{41}{66}$
    0.751(5 …)

Answers

Examination-style questions

1 a The quality of service people receive in standard class could be different to first class so it is important to have a representative number of passengers from each class.
b 32 standard class, 8 first class
c Age

2 37.5%

Section 2

1 122

2 a $500 - 45x$
b $500 - 45x = 365$
$45x = 135$
$x = 3$

3 a $\frac{1}{2} + \frac{1}{3} = \frac{5}{6}$
$\frac{1}{2} + \frac{1}{4} = \frac{3}{4}$
$\frac{1}{3} + \frac{1}{4} = \frac{7}{12}$
b i $\frac{1}{2} + \frac{1}{8}$
ii Cut each loaf in half.
Give each worker one of the halves.
Cut each of the remaining two halves into quarters.
Give each worker one of the quarters.
c $\frac{1}{2} + \frac{1}{4}$. Cut each loaf in half and give each worker one of the halves.
Cut the remaining two halves in half and give the workers one piece each.

4 40

5 a 33.5 cm
b 59.5 kg
c 14.5 litres
d £54.50

6 $\frac{2}{15}$

7 Yes, 1.9 min < 3 min

8 a i $6\frac{1}{2}, 8, 9\frac{1}{2}$
ii No, $n = 53\frac{1}{3}$ which is not an integer.
b $4n - 1$

9 9 tins for one week. He needs to buy 33 tins to have four weeks worth. $33 \times 5p = £1.65$

10 x could be 14, 21.
y could be 77 or 91.
$x + y$ could be 91, 105, 98 or 112.

11 a $3 \times 3 \times 7$
b 9
c $2 \times 2 \times 3 \times 3 \times 5 \times 5$

12 $-2, -1, 0, 1, 2, 3$

13

	A2B Cabs	Sapphire Taxis
Cinema	£58.60	£56.20
Exhibition	£51.20	£54.40
Show	£57	£63

So, the cheapest option will be to go to an exhibition and use A2B Cabs.

14 a $a = 2, b = 3$
b $-\frac{2}{3}$

15 a $a = 7$
b $d = 2\frac{1}{3}$

16 a 12
b $l = 2w + 12$
c 15 kg

17 a x^5
b x^4
c x^6
d $6x^5$

18 a $(x-3)(x+3) \equiv x^2 - 9$
$(x-3)(x+3) \equiv x^2 - 3x + 3x - 9$
So
$(x-3)(x+3) \equiv x^2 - 9$
b $\frac{x^2 - 9}{x + 3} = \frac{(x-3)(x+3)}{(x+3)} = (x-3)$

19 4, 6 and 12

20 a $5x(2 - 3x)$
b $(5x - 6)(x + 1)$

21 a Gradient of L1 $= \frac{-12}{12} = -1$. The intercept with the y axis is 12. As $y = mx + c$, $y = -1x + 12$ which is $y = -x + 12$
b $y = \frac{3}{2}x + 2$

22 a $10r + 8b$
b $r = 8$ points, $b = -2$ points, so Charlie wins with 82 points.

23 $x = 0.5, y = 3$

24 $x = 5, y = 2$ so the greatest possible value of $2x - y = 8$

25 a

1^3	1	= 1	= 1^2	= 1^2
$1^3 + 2^3$	1 + 8	= 9	= $(1 + 2)^2$	= 3^2
$1^3 + 2^3 + 3^3$	1 + 8 + 27	= 36	= $(1 + 2 + 3)^2$	= 6^2
$1^3 + 2^3 + 3^3 + 4^3$	1 + 8 + 27 + 64	= 100	= $(1 + 2 + 3 + 4)^2$	= 10^2
$1^3 + 2^3 + 3^3 + 4^3 + 5^3$	1 + 8 + 27 + 64 + 125	= 225	= $(1 + 2 + 3 + 4 + 5)^2$	= 15^2
$1^3 + 2^3 + 3^3 + 4^3 + 5^3 + 6^3$	1 + 8 + 27 + 64 + 125 + 216	= 441	= $(1 + 2 + 3 + 4 + 5 + 6)^2$	= 21^2

b 1^2, 3^2, 6^2, or squares of triangle numbers.
c Squares of the first three triangle numbers: $\left(\frac{n(n-1)}{2}\right)^2$
d 8, 27, 64, 125, 216; 2^3, 3^3, 4^3, 5^3, 6^3; $(n+1)^3$
e $(1 + 2 + 3 + 4 + 5 + 6 + 7 + 8 + 9 + 10)^2 = 55^2 = 3025$

26 $y = 4x - 5$

27 a i 0.9×10^4 **ii** 8.5×10^{-3}
b 1 and 3, 2 and 5, 3 and 7, 4 and 9

28 a 20   **b** $\frac{2\sqrt{5}}{5}$

29 $x = \frac{(2y - 8)}{(3y - 20)}$

30 $2x + \frac{1}{x} = 3$
$2x^2 - 3x + 1 = 0$
$(2x - 1)(x - 1) = 0$
Lipin is thinking of $\frac{1}{2}$ or 1.

Examination-style questions

1 $C = £600$ $d = 120$ $m = £20$

2 number of rations left = 1050
new total of rations = 1680
new number of people = 84
number of days left = 40

3 a $\frac{24}{35}$, if n = even, then $n + 1$ = odd; even × odd = even. If n = odd then $n + 1$ = even; odd × even = even.
b $2\frac{7}{20}$ **c** 2

Section 3

1 a $\frac{75}{120} = \frac{5}{8}$
b 1 h 42 min

2

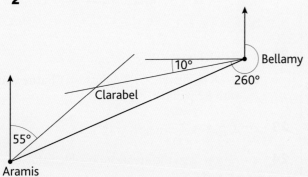

3 28

4 42 cm

5 $x = 55°$; $y = 35°$

6 a underweight   **b** 8.71 kg

7 a i Yes   **ii** 1 : 6.3   **b** 6.1%

8 12 cm²

9 $2x^2 + 5x$

10 192.9 cm²

Answers

11 a Draw parallel through PQ.

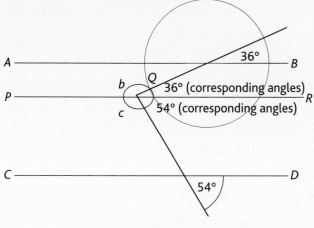

$a = 36° + 54° = 90°$

b $b + c = 270°$
$b = \frac{8}{15} \times 270° = 144°$
$144° + 36° = 180°$, so PQ is straight and must be parallel to AB and CD.

12 18

13 a 0.125 **b** $\frac{2}{5}$ **c** $\frac{2y}{x}$

14 (10, 6)

15 18 cm³

16 120°

17 a $x = 3\frac{1}{2}$ **b** $x = \frac{10}{13}$

18 431.8 cm²

19 a $c^2 + 2c - 15$
b $y = \frac{8x}{w + 8}$

20 £171 000 or £170 000

21 a $2x^2 + 5x + 3$
b 23 cm by 11 cm (by putting $x = 10$)

22 108 cm³

23 a $r^2 + 4r + 4 - (r^2 + 2r + 1) = 2r + 3$
b area of middle band = $\pi((r + 1)^2 - r^2)$
$= \pi(2r + 1)$
area of outer band = $\pi((r + 2)^2 - (r + 1)^2)$
$= \pi(2r + 3)$
$\pi(2r + 3) - \pi(2r + 1) = 2\pi$

24 176.4 m

25 A is $x^2 + 9$
B is $(x + 3)^2 = x^2 + 6x + 9$
So the difference is $6x$.

Examination-style questions

1 35 mph

2 Approximately 50 squares,
so area = 50 × 4 = 200 m²
200 m² @ £2.03 = £406

Section 4

1.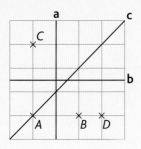

2. Shape A. $1\,m^2$ is $100\,cm \times 100\,cm = 10\,000\,cm^2$ so $0.28\,m^2$ is $2800\,cm^2$.

3. $x = 54°$

4. **a** Student's own drawing
   b 82 m

5. 3 : 2

6.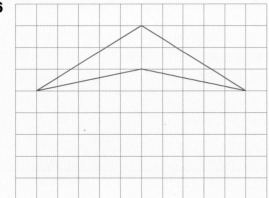

7. rotation 90° anticlockwise about O or translation 7 left 1 down

8. **a** and **b**

    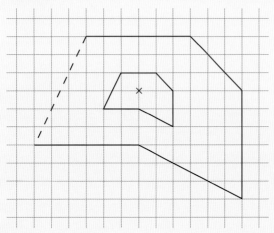

    c 3

9. **a** perimeter = 30 cm; area = 30 cm²
   b $x = 6$ cm; $y = 8$ cm
   Working must include: $6^2 + 8^2 = 10^2$ and $\frac{1}{2} \times 6 \times 8 = 6 + 8 + 10$

10. **a** 50 mph   **b** 24 minutes

11. $AC = x + 4$

12. 96 seconds

13. **a** and **b**

    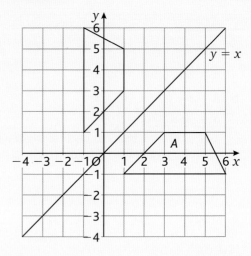

14. Melissa is not correct. The surface area is 376 cm². (Or an explanation that two side faces of 5×6 (60 cm²) replace half front and back faces of 6×8 (96 cm²) thus reducing surface area by 36 cm².)

15. **a** $120 \div 5.2 = 23.08$ **b** 29.4%

16. $x = 2.66$ (2 d.p.)

17. Tim is definitely right because any solution between 2.641 and 2.648 will be rounded to 2.6 (1 d.p.).
    For Sara there is not enough information to tell. Any solution greater than 2.641 and less than 2.645 rounds to 2.64 but any solution greater than or equal to 2.645 and less than 2.648 rounds to 2.65. So it could be either 2.64 or 2.65

18. $7^2 + 7^2 = 98$ and $10^2 = 100$
    The triangle is not right-angled so it cannot be drawn inside a semicircle.
    $40^2 + 9^2 = 1681 = 41^2$
    The triangle is right-angled so it can be drawn inside the semicircle.

19. **a** 1 g costs $\frac{85}{150} = 0.5666\ldots$
    b percentage increase = 15.6%

20. 23.77 cm²

21. 86.9 cm²

22 a 4 m

b $x = 20$ gives $y = 4$, the height of the dish or $x = 10$ gives $y = 0$, so $B = (10, 0)$ and $C = (20, 4)$

c (10, 6.25)

23 $x = 76°$ and $y = 64°$

24 a $\frac{1}{v} = \frac{1}{f} - \frac{1}{u}$

$\frac{1}{v} = \frac{u - f}{uf}$

Taking reciprocals gives the required answer, $v = \frac{uf}{u - f}$

b Substituting $u = 2f$ gives $v = \frac{2f^2}{f} = 2f = u$

25 9.1%

26 a i angle $RAB = x$

ii angle $BCP = 2x$

b angle $ABC = 180° - 2x$
angle $ABR = 90° - x$
angle $ARB = 180° - (90° - x) - x = 90°$

Examination-style questions

1 a $x = 94°$

b i $y = 47°$

ii alternate segment

Section 5

1 length = $4x$; width = $3x$

2 12 100 square yards

3 a $T = 12x + 8y$ **b** 44

4 a

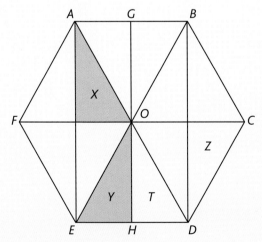

b a reflection in the line OH

5 a 150 ml of water is added to the glass.

b 1 : 3

c 9 s

6

7 10 : 15 : 9

8 a $8x$

b $(2x + 1)^2$

9 a Andrew 22 pass; Bill 28 pass; Clare 13 fail

b 1 not attempted (-10); 3 correct ($+15$); 6 incorrect (-12) $-10 + 15 - 12 = -7$

10 a sum of angles in quadrilateral = 360°
360 − 3 × 90 = 90
So if three angles are 90° the fourth angle must also be 90°.

b Sum of angles in a hexagon = 720°
720° − 5 × 90° = 270°
So if five of the angles are 90° the sixth angle is 270°.
So, a hexagon can be drawn with five right angles.

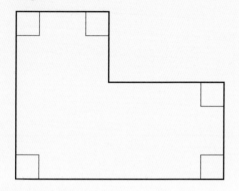

11 (2, 1)

12 a Both lengths are $\sqrt{(1^2 + 2^2)}$

b

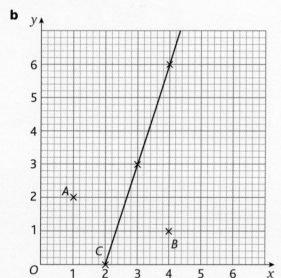

13 $A: x$ $B: x + 2$ $C: 3x + 6$ $D: 5x$ $E: 5x + 4$
$A + B + C + D = 10x + 8$
$2 \times E = 2(5x + 4) = 10x + 8$

14 3.7

15 Approximately 16:30

16 360

17 a i

v (km/h)	0	15	30	45	60	75	90	105	120
d (metres)	0	4.5	12	22.5	36	52.5	72	94.5	120

ii

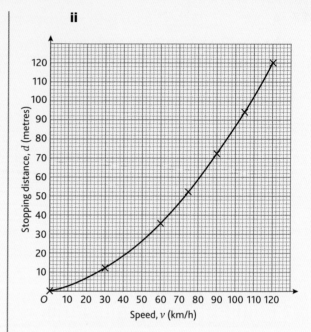

b i 160 metres

ii No, it was travelling at 120 km/h, which is 7.5 km/h above the speed limit.

18 a 96 cm³

b correctly completed table with sensibly chosen numbers leading to an answer of 6.6 cm (1 d.p.)

19 a $x = 6.5$ cm

b For a gradient of 4, the base of the ladder needs to be 1.8 ÷ 4 = 0.45 m from the wall. Using Pythagoras, the ladder is actually 0.87 (2 d.p.) from the wall. So, it is **not** safe.

c $h = 10.4$ (1 d.p.)

20 interior angle of a pentagon =
180° − 360° ÷ 5 = 108°
$\angle BAC = \angle BCA = (180° − 108°) ÷ 2 = 36°$
($\triangle ABC$ is isosceles)
$\angle EAC = \angle DCA = 108° − 36° = 72°$
$\angle EAC + \angle AED = 72° + 108° = 180°$
So $\angle EAC$ and $\angle AED$ are allied angles and AC is parallel to ED.
ED is the side of a regular pentagon.
AC is the longest side of the isosceles $\triangle ABC$.
So $AC \neq ED$
The fact that AC and ED are parallel and not equal in length shows that $ACDE$ is a trapezium.

21 40.5 cm (1 d.p.)

22 a 24 ÷ 8 = 3
17.5 ÷ 5 = 3.5
Both of these scale factors need to be the same for the enlarged photo to fit exactly.

b The 8 cm side needs to be cropped to 6.8 cm long.

Answers

23 a Student's accurate scale drawing of the field

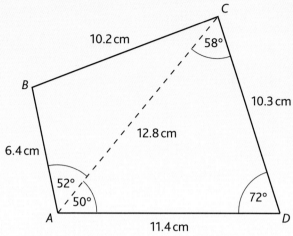

Scale: 1 cm represents 1 m

b

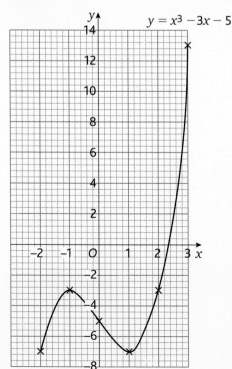

c Billy runs along the dotted black line in the drawing above for distance 146 metres at a speed of 4.8 to 4.9 metres per second.

24 a

x	−2	−1	0	1	2	3
y	−7	−3	−5	−7	−3	13

b

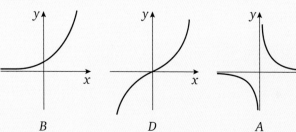

c 2.8

25 £1.30

26 a $7^2 = 49$ and $3^2 + 5^2 = 34$
These are not equal so the triangle is not right-angled.

b Side opposite x is 5. Side opposite y is 3. The bigger angle is opposite the bigger side.

c iii $\dfrac{\sin x}{5} = \dfrac{\sin y}{3}$

27 a $2w^2 + 4w + 2 = 2(w^2 + 2w + 1)$

b $8x$

c $\dfrac{1}{x-1} + \dfrac{1}{x+1} = \dfrac{x+1}{(x-1)(x+1)} = \dfrac{x-1}{(x-1)(x+1)} = \dfrac{x+1+x-1}{(x-1)(x+1)} = \dfrac{2x}{x^2 - x + x - 1} = \dfrac{2x}{x^2 - 1}$

28 a $\angle BXC = \angle AXD$ (vertically opposite angles)
$\angle DBC = \angle CAD$ (angles subtended from chord CD)
$\angle BCA = \angle BDA$ (angles subtended from chord AB)
$BX \neq DX$
Corresponding angles in $\triangle BXC$ and in $\triangle AXD$ are equal but the lengths are not equal.
So $\triangle BXC$ and $\triangle AXD$ are similar.

b 10.5 cm

c 10.3 cm (1 d.p.)

29 6 mm

30 148.9°

31 $\vec{AD} = \begin{pmatrix} 3 \\ 1 \end{pmatrix} + \begin{pmatrix} 2 \\ -5 \end{pmatrix} + \begin{pmatrix} -5 \\ -2 \end{pmatrix} = \begin{pmatrix} 0 \\ -6 \end{pmatrix}$

There is no movement horizontally from A to D so D is vertically below A.

32

x	5	10	0.5
y	5	1.25	500

33 a $6a - 6b$

b $a + b$

c $5a + 5b$

d O, S and R lie on a straight line.
Length of OS is five times the length of OR.

34 a

    B   D   A

b i The maximum value of y is 1 not 0.5 and/or the minimum value of y is -0.5 not -1.

  ii $y = 0.5 \sin x$

35 $9.11 \, \text{cm}^2$

36 1312π or 4121.77 litres (2 d.p.)

37 AB is parallel to CD (alternate angles).
$\vec{CD}$ is parallel to $\vec{AB}$ so $\vec{CD}$ is a multiple of $\vec{AB}$.
$\vec{CD} = 4\vec{AB}$ so $k = 4 \times 5 = 20$

38 a translation by $\begin{pmatrix} 0 \\ -4 \end{pmatrix}$

  b stretch parallel to y-axis, scale factor 2

  c translation by $\begin{pmatrix} -1 \\ 0 \end{pmatrix}$

39 $(1\tfrac{1}{2}, 4)$

40 translation by $\begin{pmatrix} 0 \\ 8 \end{pmatrix}$

41 4

42 a $x\left(\dfrac{18.4 - 2x}{2}\right) = 21$; multiply by 2:
$18.4x - 2x^2 = 42$; multiply by 2.5:
$5x^2 - 46x + 105 = 0$

  b length = 5 cm, width = 4.2 cm

Examination-style questions

1 If the triangle is isosceles, two angles must be equal and all the angles must add up to 180°. So either $4x = 80°$ or $x = 80°$

If you take $4x = 80°$ then $x = 20°$, so the angles would be 20°, 80° and 80°, which adds up to 180°.

(If you had taken $x = 80°$ first, then the angles would be 80°, 80° and 320°, which does not add up to 180°. You would then have had to try the other value of x.)

2 The length scale factor is 2 so the height of B is 20 cm.

3 21.7 cm (1 d.p.)

4 15